EVERYBODY'S GOLF BOOK

EVERYBODY'S GOLF BOOK

Juan "Chi Chi" Rodriguez

with **Chuck Fitt**

illustrations by **Simon Paukov**

Prepared by **Elias Productions, Inc.**

The Viking Press   New York

I dedicate this book to the thousands of PGA "home" professionals who work untiringly to help country club members and public course players to become better golfers so they may enjoy the great game of golf more.

Chi Chi

First published in 1975 by The Viking Press, Inc.
625 Madison Avenue, New York, N.Y. 10022

Published simultaneously in Canada by
The Macmillan Company of Canada Limited

Library of Congress Cataloging in Publication Data

Rodriguez, Juan, 1936–
Everybody's golf book.

1. Golf. I. Title.
GV965.R573 1975   796.352′3   74–30272
ISBN 0–670–30036–5

Printed in U.S.A.

FOREWORD

I have had the opportunity to watch Chi Chi play in many tournaments over the years and consider him one of the finest pro golfers on the PGA circuit.

I especially respect his play because he has compensated for his size by becoming a true student of the game. He has had to make adjustments in his style to make up for his 126 pounds.

He is an outstanding shotmaker, and I feel the reason is that he has one of the best grips in the game. His small hands give him a feel that many of the pros envy.

Chi Chi has all the credentials to write this excellent instruction book.

One little incident that portrays his dedication and determination sticks in my memory: After the Byron Nelson Classic in 1971 he promised me he would return after his operation on his hands and win my 1972 tournament. He did it!

Byron Nelson

CONTENTS

1 INTRODUCTION

Juan "Chi Chi" Rodriguez is acknowledged to be one of the true stylists of the game of golf. And although he is only five feet seven and 125 pounds, he consistently raps a ball off the tee as far as Jack Nicklaus, Tom Weiskopf, and the other big hitters in the game. This ability to hit the long ball, as well as to finesse any kind of shot, has added so much to his scope as a teacher that he is considered one of the greatest in the game.

Not too long ago *Esquire* magazine picked Chi Chi among the top ten teachers in golf. The choice drew applause from among the touring professionals, many of whom come to Rodriguez when their game goes sour.

Of course, the little man with the big grin has been over the route himself. As a poor boy in Puerto Rico, he began caddying at the age of six. And he actually learned to play golf with clubs fashioned out of guava tree limbs and with tin cans hammered into the shape of golf balls.

Proceeding from this start, he eventually won his first PGA title (the Denver Open) in 1963. Since then he has captured many championships on the rugged PGA tour, including the Lucky International, the Western Open, and the Byron Nelson Classic. Almost every year he's in the top twenty among the money winners, and he has earned well over $750,000 on the tour since his first year in 1962.

Chi Chi is the first to admit that he was blessed with great teachers as he was getting his game off the ground. Such stars as touring pros Ed Dudley and Pete Cooper took him under their wings when he was at an early age, and they worked many hours with him. Then Rusty Gilbert, a topnotch teaching pro in his day, came along to take over what the other two had started. Now Chi Chi's brother, Jesus, is carrying on as Chi Chi's instructor.

"I'll never be able to tell you how great these pros were to me," Chi Chi says. "I think that I'm able to convey my thoughts to others because of the way they have worked with me. Hour after hour they'd have me out on the practice tee. They taught me every shot in the book and made me work at it. I'll be forever grateful to them for what they did for me. Without them, I'd probably be chopping sugar cane back in my native Puerto Rico."

Chi Chi is able to draw the ball, or slice it, or hit the high,

1

floating shot, or the low screamer—it's all part of his repertoire. As one prominent touring professional put it: "He's the last of the truly great shotmakers. They just don't make his kind any more."

In addition to his shot making, Chi Chi's smallness has a lot to do with his popularity both as a player and as a teacher. He had to work harder than the average-size player; consequently he studied and allowed for all the idiosyncrasies of the game. And this hard work and concentration enabled him to get the most out of what he had to work with.

The little man with the big grin signed a million-dollar contract in 1974 with Hyatt Rio Mar, a condominium complex in Puerto Rico. Not many pros, big or little, can say this.

So if you're small, or a woman, you'll find it easy to identify yourself with Chi Chi. And if you're of average size, you can say to yourself, "If this little guy can do it, so can I."

Chi Chi tells it all in this book. He says he can knock strokes off any man's game. Follow his precepts and the lifelike line drawings illustrating his points, and you may well be happy with what happens to your score.

The Editors

2 THE START

It seems a long time ago, but actually it has been only fifteen years since I became a professional golfer. Like everybody else, I always remember the bad shots. That's human nature. The golfer remembers the bad shots so he can work on them. And since the average professional hits only three or four perfect shots —just the way he planned them—in a round, he has a lot of practicing to do.

That's the name of the game—practice. I spend at least one hour a day, every day, on the practice tee. This in addition to the many rounds I play in actual competition. But whether he's playing for the thousands of dollars now up for grabs on the pro tour, or just a casual dollar Nassau, the one aim in every golfer's mind is establishing a correct, powerful, grooved swing.

This can be stated emphatically: It is impossible for any golfer to play any kind of consistent game without a swing that can be repeated.

How, then, do you go about building a swing that you can count on in any kind of weather and under all kinds of pressure? The lessons I'm going to pass on to you I have learned through laborious trial and error—watching other players, experimenting with various grips, discarding the bad and keeping the good, continually searching for better ways to execute a stroke—until now I feel that I have all the tools necessary to make you a better golfer. To put it bluntly, you are going to get the benefit of the knowledge I have picked up in devoting most of my waking hours since childhood to practice and play on a golf course, from thousands of rounds of golf—the game from which I make my living.

As I see it, there's nothing really difficult about golf. And I can see no reason whatever that anyone shouldn't play in the 70s. I know you're shocked at this, but I'm sincere in my belief. Some way or another, Mr. 15-Handicapper throws up mental barriers that restrict his game. He'll say he can't hit a long shot. Or his irons won't go in the direction he pointed them. Or he hasn't got the skill or coordination to execute a full swing.

But he'll tell you that chipping and putting are a different matter. He'll say that if he doesn't take a full swing, he has control of his club. Yet if he just thought about this, the full swing is just an extension of the short swing. Sure, like anything else, it takes some learning. But, in my opinion, the correct movements in any swing are a hundred times less difficult than he thinks. In fact, once you get on the right track, doing things the right way takes a lot less effort than doing things the wrong way.

I agree that some people do things and learn more easily than others. What really gets me is watching a golfer sweating over his shots on a practice tee to no constructive purpose. Sure, he loves the game. But watching him do things he probably has done wrong all his life just galls me. If he stands out there on that tee until he's a hundred years old, he'll just keep making the same old mistakes again and again. In fact, he's going to get worse and worse because the bad habits will irritate him and the utter frustration of not being able to improve will wear him down.

I know that thousands of golfers console themselves by saying that at least the game gives them exercise and companionship. That's great. But every golfer really feels at the bottom of his heart that he can play better. And he can. It's going to take application, thought, and effort, but the golfer who goes about learning the right way will play that way the rest of his life. As everyone knows, the greatest pleasure in life is mastering anything. And in this game of golf, a sport you can play for almost as long as you can walk, what better satisfaction is there than improving?

Before we really get under way, let me explain what we're doing and what we hope to achieve. As we go from chapter to chapter, we will be presenting one or two fundamentals to the golfer for him to work on and polish, so he will be building a sound foundation as we go along. The golfer who devotes just a half hour of practice a day to each of these points will find that his game improves. And I don't mean in the future. *I mean immediately!*

His degree of progress, of course, will be entirely up to him. But if he continues to practice and continues to apply the basics as we go along, I guarantee that I'll take from ten to fifteen strokes off any golfer's game. I'm talking about the golfer who is shooting in the 90s.

Of course, he will have to follow instructions. He'll thus be able to eliminate the bad habits and pick up the good. And another thing—we're certainly not attempting to cover all phases of the game, or even one hundredth—of this unlimited subject. We'll just concern ourselves with the basics that have checked out over the years—basics that can be checked and counterchecked, not simply left to imagination and haphazard guesswork.

I know I haven't got the picture swing of a Sam Snead, who was taken into the PGA Hall of Fame in 1953 and is still playing in tournaments in his sixties. I know I don't have that fluid movement, but I get results, and that's what counts. As I see it, some measures that long were considered the basics of a sound swing are not really as important as they were once believed to be. Other things, which weren't even considered important years ago, hit me as being invaluable, the fundamentals of the modern golf swing.

Another thing—I don't believe in setting up rigid rules for everyone to go by. I advocate the type of teaching that stresses the nature and feel of a specific player. But one thing is sure—we'll all be going in the same direction, and when we're finished, we'll all arrive at the same conclusion.

For instance, I'm not going to tell you something and then skip over to another point without first exploring all the angles of the first point. We're going through this step by step. In these lessons our method will stress what you're supposed to do to reach the results we're after. The actions that cause the results—these are the true basics of golf. For despite the different mannerisms and personal touches that distinguish us all as individuals, I never in my life have seen a great player whose method of striking the ball did *not* include the fundamentals that we will emphasize.

Remember—you have to be comfortable. Golf is *not* a life-or-death situation. It's just a game and should be treated as such. So stay loose, and we'll be on our way with the first lesson—the grip.

3 THE GRIP

Good golf begins with a good grip. I know this statement has about as much oomph as a wet dishrag hitting a sink. For the average man-on-the-street golfer, the grip is the least glamorous part of the entire swing. He sees it as accomplishing nothing decisive. But, to the professional golfer, a good grip is the actual heartbeat of the swing.

This is only logical. The player's only contact with the ball is through the clubhead. And his only direct physical contact with the club is through his hands. In the golf swing the power is originated by movements of the body. As this power generates and builds, it is transferred from the body to the arms, which, in turn, transfer it through the hands to the clubhead.

To put it simply, the clubhead is likened to the last person on a crack-the-whip line—it's going hundreds of times faster than the element that originated the velocity. And, of course, this chain action depends strictly on the grip. With a defective grip, there's no way a golfer can hold the club securely at the top of his backswing. And if the club isn't under the control of a good grip, the power a golfer generates with his body will never reach the clubhead.

There are three types of grips—the overlapping, or Vardon; the interlocking, and the baseball. I use the Vardon grip, so, for reasons of expediency, we'll teach the overlapping, or Vardon, grip. Now don't get me wrong—some pretty fair cashers use the other grips. Jack Nicklaus, for example, goes with interlocking, and Bob Rosburg and Art Wall, Jr., like the baseball grip. But if you use the interlocking grip or the baseball grip, it won't make any difference. Basically, you'll be doing the same thing as if you used the Vardon grip.

In a good, solid grip both hands work as a unit. To cite the most common fault of the average amateur: A right-hander kills any chance for a cohesive union of both hands if he lets the right hand dominate the swing at the start or at any time during the swing. One essential, then, to insure a good two-handed grip is to get both hands on the club with just the right amount of firmness.

Now remember, we're not killing snakes, and we're not holding on for dear life. It's the relaxed grip I'm talking about. Just pretend you're holding a little bird. You don't want it to get away, and

TEN-FINGER (BASEBALL) OVERLAP (VARDON) INTERLOCK

you don't want to squeeze it to death. That's the firm, relaxed grip. So let's proceed:

Put the club in the general position it would be in at address. With the back of your left hand facing the target, place the club in the left hand so that the shaft is pressed against the muscular pad at the inside heel of the palm, and the shaft lies directly across the top joint of the left forefinger.

Crook the forefinger around the shaft and you will find you can lift the club rather easily and maintain a firm grip by supporting it just with the muscles of that finger and the pad of the heel. Now close the fingers and then the thumb, and the club should be where it's supposed to be.

When you have completed this left-handed grip, the V formed by the thumb and forefinger should point to your right eye. The total pressure of all fingers should be the same. The main pressure points are the last three fingers, with the forefinger and the palm pad assisting. The three fingers press up, the pad presses down, and the shaft is locked in. Keeping pressure on the palm pad does three things—it strengthens the left arm throughout the swing; at the top of the backswing this pressure prevents the club from slipping; and it acts as a firm reinforcement at impact.

This pressure I'm speaking of should be alive, the kind of pressure you can feel. And be relaxed with it. Some golfers grab a club so tight it looks as if they were going to tear off the leather. But there's no need for this. In fact, an overgrip is a hazard in that when you overgrip you automatically tighten the cords in your arm, and it becomes so stiff that the arm won't react the way a relaxed arm should.

Too tight a grip will also knock your wrists out of action, since they, too, won't react to the drive of your body. A secure and comfortable grip is what you're after. Then the weight of the clubhead will automatically tighten your fingers on the shaft.

Now let's join forces with the right hand. This will be a little

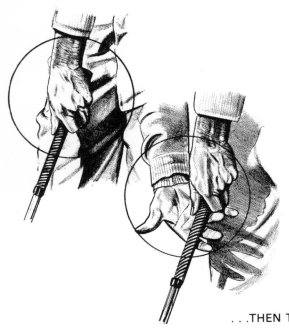

THE VARDON (OVERLAPPING) GRIP
STARTS LIKE ANY OTHER . . .
BY PLACING THE LEFT HAND
ON THE CLUB SHAFT . . .

. . .THEN THE FINGERS OF THE RIGHT HAND . . .

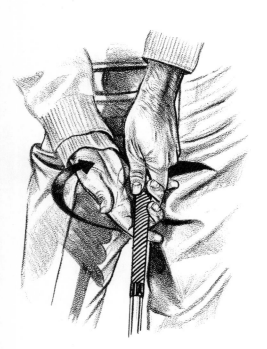

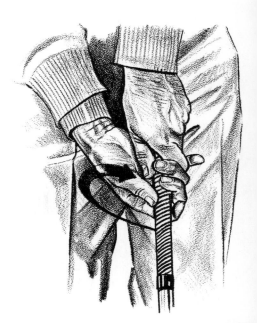

BRING THE RIGHT HAND AROUND . . .   . . . AND TURN THE LEFT HAND IN

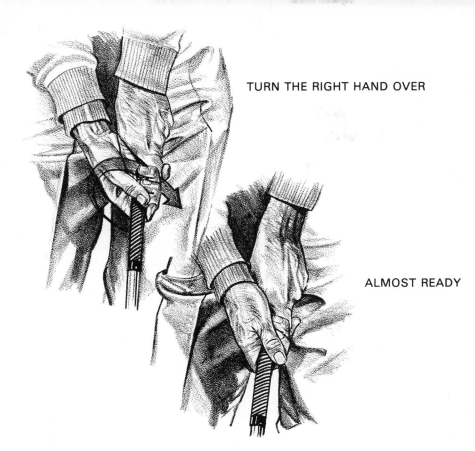

TURN THE RIGHT HAND OVER

ALMOST READY

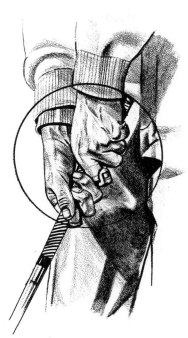

NOT TOO TIGHT . . .
JUST AS IF YOU WERE
HOLDING A BIRD AND
DIDN'T WANT IT TO GET AWAY

more complicated, since the tendency is for the right forefinger and the thumb to dominate the swing. If they do, you're a dead duck. These pincer fingers, the forefinger and thumb, are no good at all in helping you build a good grip and powerful swing. The reason is that the muscles of the forefinger and thumb connect with the powerful set of muscles that run along the outside of the right elbow. If you work the tips of the thumb and forefinger, you automatically activate these big muscles. And these are *not* the muscles you want activated in a smooth and effortless golf swing. Using these muscles is what causes all the lurching and lunging you see at all golf courses across the country.

To obtain the proper grip with the right hand, hold the hand out flat with the palm facing the target. Your left hand is in position. Place the club in your right hand so that the shaft lies across the top joint of the four fingers and well below the palm.

The right-hand grip is a finger grip. The two fingers supplying the pressure are the two in the middle. As we said before, relax the thumb and the forefinger. Now, what to do with the little finger? Well, just slide it across the forefinger of the left hand and it automatically locks itself between the left forefinger and the middle finger. Next simply fold the right hand over your left thumb. When you have done this, the right thumb should ride down the left side of the shaft, but just slightly.

The main thing you must remember about the right hand: THE CLUB MUST BE IN THE FINGERS AND NOT—I REPEAT, NOT—IN THE PALM. The ball must be hit sharply, and to do this the player must transmit the greatest speed to the clubhead. *Controlled speed* is what we're after, and you can get this control only through the fingers.

That little finger on the right hand riding between the left forefinger and the middle finger may seem awkward at first. But the idea behind this is to keep your hands from slipping apart. Also it gives the feeling of your two hands being one unit working together.

Also there's the thumb area of the right hand. To have the perfect right-handed grip that's strong where it's supposed to be, here's a little tip: When you're taking the grip, make sure the two V's—one on each hand—are pressed tightly together. Keep them pressed together when you fold your right hand over your left.

I know I have it "right" when the big knuckle on the back of my right hand is pressing to the left, toward the target. The knuckle rides almost on top of the shaft. If it does, I know that the fingers are in control. And here's another indication that you've got the club in the correct grip: When you fold over the right hand, the left thumb will fit perfectly into the cup formed by the palm of the right hand.

The togetherness of the left and right thumbs strengthens the feeling of oneness you should have when you start your back-swing. It's when you reach the top of your backswing that a poor grip will collapse. So before you start the clubhead back, check your right-handed grip and make sure the V formed by the thumb and forefinger is pointing to the bottom of your chin.

Another word on those two villains of the right hand—the thumb and forefinger: While the tips of the forefinger and thumb serve the pro golfer as finesse fingers, learning to use them requires some attention. And you have to develop this as you go along. However, at the beginning of your career as a golfer you should forget about putting pressure on the forefinger and thumb of your right hand.

Another tip for the beginner: Grip the club and swing it entirely with the forefinger and thumb disengaged. You'll get the feeling that should carry over when you grip the club with both hands—that the thumb and forefinger are hardly on the shaft of the club.

About the V's. A lot of beginners think that if the two V's are pointed correctly their grip must be right. This isn't so. The direction of the V's is no guarantee; it's just one way of checking. This is why you can't say too much about the grip. Once you learn the correct way, you'll be able to forget about it entirely—your hands will automatically fall into place. The reason for this is that the correct grip brings into play the correct muscles of your arms and body.

What we've gone into up to now is, as I said before, not an iron-clad situation—we're not all built alike. Take me: I'm five feet seven and weigh about 125 pounds. I have to cheat a little with my right thumb. In other words, I have to turn it over to the right so I'll get more power. But it took me a long time to control this change, and I wouldn't recommend it to anyone just getting into the game.

If, when we get all the basics laid out, you feel that you can use more power, then go to a pro and tell him your problem. He'll be glad to work with you in straightening it out. The fortunate golfer is the one who needs to make only minor adjustments as he's going for the goal of shooting in the 70s.

One more thing on the grip. Some pros—and I'll admit doing it myself—use what is called the short thumb. In other words, I'll pull up, or crinkle, my thumb on the left hand to get just a little better grip on the shaft. Of course, this should be strictly in the pros' thinking area.

Now, with the help of the line drawings that accompany this chapter on the grip, I'd like you to practice your grip for at least fifteen minutes a day. I know what you're going to say: "Just the grip for fifteen minutes a day?" Yes, that's right. Practice the grip until it comes automatically, so you don't have to think about it every time you pick up a club.

One other thing I was going to get into was the grip to use if you want to draw or slice the ball. But, after thinking about it, I realized it also involves the stance. So we'll take that up after the next chapter, which, incidentally, *is* on the stance.

Work on the grip. And I'll be back with you in the next chapter.

THE STANCE

There is only one way to generate the speed you need for power, and that is by having the proper stance before you attempt to swing the club. Again, the prime factor in selecting a stance has to be complete comfort. But there's another factor, too: Which stance will allow the biggest body turn?

There are three basic stances: the square, the closed, and the open. In the square stance you place your feet directly along the intended flight of your shot. Point the toes slightly out and distribute your weight evenly. In the closed stance, the main difference is that you drop the right foot slightly behind the left one, away from the line of flight. But just slightly. This, in effect, causes the hips and body to swing somewhat to the right. In the open stance your left foot is slightly drawn back from the intended line of flight, causing the hips and body to face somewhat to the left.

I use a slightly open stance, drawing my left foot back a bit from the imaginary line of flight. My right foot is about an inch beyond the outside of my right shoulder. This is better for smaller golfers like me because I use quite a bit of leg movement and need maximum stability.

Remember what I said in the chapter on The Start? About my experimenting with different ways of doing things? Well, it took me a long time to arrive at this position. But since I finally found out that this was the best one for me, I've stuck to it all the way. However, for the average golfer, I suggest a square stance with the feet no farther apart than the shoulders. Anything wider might restrict a full shoulder and hip turn.

Many golfers make the big mistake of regarding the stance as that preparatory part of the swing in which the player just lines himself up on the target he's shooting at. While one of the func-

OPEN STANCE . . . SQUARE . . . AND THE CLOSED

DRIVER
THE BALL IS TEED UP MIDWAY
OF THE FEET. NOTE THAT THE
LEFT FOOT IS POINTED AT
ABOUT A QUARTER OF A TURN

LOFTED CLUB
YOU'RE RELAXED, WITH THE KNEES
SLIGHTLY FLEXED. YOU'RE USING
A LOFTED CLUB, SO YOU'RE PLAYING
THE BALL OFF THE RIGHT HEEL

tions of the stance *is* to get on target, it also has a few other aspects that are more important.

Power and control must be combined in a good golf swing, and in the stance the golfer sets himself so that his body will be in balance throughout the swing; his muscles are ready to move smoothly, and therefore all the energy he pours into the swing will result in maximum control and power.

When you watch a fine player addressing the ball with his little mannerisms of moving the club, sighting down the fairway, and getting himself settled, don't interpret these movements as nervousness. What he's actually trying to do is feel that everything he will be doing in his swing is poised and in balance.

When a golfer steps up to his ball to play a shot, he first lines up the face of his club with the target. He then aligns himself with the face of his club. The adjustment of the hands, arms, body, feet, and legs is done simultaneously and interdependently. But, for the purpose of pointing out the various foot positions, we'll go at this slowly.

First, how far apart should your feet be? As I said earlier in the chapter, your feet should be no farther apart than your shoulders. Ah, but there are variations of this. A good rule to follow is that you play the woods and long irons the same—with the feet and shoulders the same. Then, as you go up the line to your more lofted clubs, you inch your feet closer together.

Again, getting back to the direction my feet are pointing in, I use the slightly open stance, with my right foot at a right angle to the line of flight and the left foot turned slightly in. Now I'm in a sort of pigeon-toed position, and I *don't* recommend this to all golfers.

Because of my extremely hard downswing, my left foot serves as a brace. And I really plant that left one. In fact, I like to feel that I've nailed it to the ground. It keeps me from losing my balance and actually falling.

But getting back to the basics for the average golfer. Keep your right foot at right angles to the line of flight and open your left foot about a quarter of a turn, or whatever is most comfortable for you. The term "quarter of a turn" is probably confusing. Placing your left foot at 90 degrees and right at the target would be a full turn. Just take one-quarter of 90 degrees and you've got it. When a player uses this stance, his body will be in a better position, as his club comes into the ball on the downswing, to go in the direction his left foot is going. In fact, you can tell exactly where a good golfer's ball is going by looking at his stance—or where he's aiming.

You've seen the guy get up on the tee, point both feet at 90-degree angles, and address his ball. Man, you don't know whether he's going to hit it right-handed or left-handed. His stance certainly gives you no clue as to what he's all about.

Having the basic stance accomplishes several things. First, it makes it easier for the golfer to control the muscles that initiate the swing as he draws the club back. Secondly, the correct stance acts as a governor on the amount of hip turn he should take on the backswing.

Here are some points to check when you're practicing your hip turn: When you start from the correct basic stance and complete your full hip turn, your belt buckle should be parallel with the toe of your right foot. Now, by having your left foot turned out (that quarter turn, remember?) you can get through the ball with everything you've got. The fact that an apparent little thing like the position of your left foot can affect your entire swing is just one of those things about golf. If you've got the right ingredients, you can "cook the shot."

As for the head and eyes, I always keep my head about six inches in back of the ball at address and tilted slightly to the right. I concentrate on looking at the ball throughout my backswing and downswing. It is a fallacy that the head *must* remain perfectly still on every shot. This is almost physically impossible. But you should concentrate on keeping it as still as possible.

Let's go to the arms. DURING THE SWING ONE OF THE TWO ARMS IS ALWAYS STRAIGHT—THAT IS, FULLY EXTENDED. There's a very basic reason for this: In order for the club to travel at its maximum speed, one arm must be extended at all times. If a golfer breaks his left elbow on his backswing or breaks his right elbow on his follow through, he shortens his arc. And if he swings with a shorter arc, he's going to hit the ball shorter because he isn't able to accelerate the speed of his clubhead to maximum efficiency. We'll go into this more thoroughly when we get into the next chapter, on the backswing or take-away.

But now more on the arms—or the elbows, to be exact. Both elbows should be tucked in, not sticking out from the body. At the point of address the left elbow should point to the left hipbone and the right elbow should be zeroed in on the right hipbone. That should be easy to remember . . . left elbow, left hipbone; right elbow, right hipbone. Also, there should be a feeling of fixed unity between the two forearms and the two wrists. And it should be maintained throughout the entire swing.

Another word on the elbows. You should press them as closely together as you possibly can. As you address your ball, here's another "checkpoint Charlie" for you: The pocket of the left elbow —that is, the inside middle of the elbow—should be pointing toward the right arm at about ten o'clock. In this position of address the left arm hangs straight and the right pocket should be toward the sky at about eleven o'clock. On the backswing this right elbow *must not* fly out, and it won't if positioned correctly at address. DURING THE FIRST HALF OF THE BACKSWING THE RIGHT ELBOW SHOULD MOVE HARDLY AT ALL. As it folds close to your body, the right elbow should be pointing toward the ground.

In the meantime what's the left elbow doing? At address it was hanging almost straight. It should stay this way throughout the backswing, the downswing, and throughout almost the entire shot, relaxing only after you've hit the ball.

With practice, your arms will react the same way swing after swing, almost like a machine. As your swing becomes more and more grooved, you will get the feeling that the arms and the club form one firm unit. And as you practice, your arms will recognize with increasing certainty when they're on the right track. This

ELBOW POCKETS SHOULD
POINT SLIGHTLY UP . . .
THE LEFT AT ABOUT
ELEVEN O'CLOCK AND THE
RIGHT AT TEN O'CLOCK

swing, you will come to realize, is bound to go away from the ball and come back through the ball nearly the same way each time.

Let's go into the final phase of the stance, the one involving the body and legs. Be a little more on your heels than on the balls of your feet so you are able to wiggle your toes inside your shoes. Your back is the same as when you're walking around. *Don't* crouch the shoulders over the ball. Bend your head down by bending your neck, *not* your back or shoulders. Your knees should be properly flexed, the legs supple but tensioned. The rest of the body will pick up the temper of the legs.

In addressing the ball, lower your body from an erect position into a more balanced position for executing the shot. Now bend your knees from the thighs down—DO NOT USE YOUR HIPS! As your knees bend, the upper part of your trunk remains normal and erect. In golf this sitdown motion is like lowering yourself onto a spectator sports stick. In this semi-sitting position you should feel heavy in the buttocks. Your lower legs—from the knees down—should feel springy and strong. And, as I said before, you should be more on your heels than on the balls of your feet.

As you're standing erect just before addressing the ball, the clubhead should be about four inches above the ball. As you lower yourself into the semi-sitting position, your upper trunk should feel like an elevator dropping down a floor—the clubhead drops as you drop. When you have completed your stance, the clubhead should be about an inch above the ball. Then the hands do the rest.

Now, during the start of the swing, the knees should work toward each other. In view of this, each knee should be pointing in. This is a short cut, so to speak, since, as you don't have to move your knees as much, you can concentrate on other things about your swing.

The right knee should point in slightly more than the left. This helps brace the right leg on the backswing. This is a *must,* since the right leg must be planted to prevent the golfer from swaying to the right as he takes the club back. And another thing, the right knee is thus in a position for the downswing when the power of the right hip and leg is released. The left knee pointing in just a little at address is the best insurance for developing proper left-leg action on both backswing and downswing.

By this time you're probably wondering how in the world you can get any power into a swing by using the so-called weak muscles, or inside muscles. Certainly you're not bringing into play those powerful outside arm and shoulder muscles that are supposed to supply all the power in all sports. Ah, but that's the key —golf isn't a power game; it's finesse, a matter of putting the right pressures here and there. Coordination, concentration, and complete commitment . . . those are the answers to a complete golf game.

So, before we break into the next chapter—which, by the way, will be on the take-away, or backswing—let's review this chapter on stance. You're standing upright at your ball; your feet are never farther apart than your shoulders; your back is straight as you bend to the ball from the base of the neck; your left arm is hanging straight and fully extended; the right arm is slightly bent, ready to fold correctly on the backswing; your knees are slightly turned in; and your eyes are on the ball. You are in the classic address position, but more than that, you sense that you're perfectly on balance and ready to work freely and fluidly. Rhythm and balance are with you.

Go back to the first chapter and try out the grip again. Then, start taking the stance. The next time around we're going into the take-away. See you then.

5 THE TAKE-AWAY

The basic fundamentals of the take-away are smoothness and complete lack of hurry. First you grip the club, then take your stance (as in the previous two chapters), and then you waggle. As we've said before, the waggle isn't an outlet for nervousness. It's simply the only way of getting comfortable. It's a sort of rhythmic cadence that gets you into the proper frame of mind to hit the ball with a smooth and effortless swing.

Another thing that is very important at this juncture: WHEN YOU MOVE THE CLUBHEAD AWAY FROM THE BALL ON THE BACKSWING (OR TAKE-AWAY), MOVE IT THE SAME WAY EACH TIME. This pattern should never vary. You're taking the clubhead away from the ball in a straight line *each* time. Once you learn to coil your body on the take-away and uncoil it on the downswing in cadence, you're in the groove you've been searching for.

So now you're over the ball, have the proper grip on the club, are in the desired stance, and you waggle the club. Then begins the slow, completely unhurried take-away to the top of the backswing. If the player executes properly, at the top of the backswing his legs, arms, hips, shoulders, and hands are properly poised for the big movement—the downswing.

Of course, the foundation of the golf swing is footwork and balance. At address your weight should not be on the balls of the feet but should be shaded toward the heels and evenly distributed on the inside of each foot. On the backswing, about 75 to 80 per cent of your weight shifts to the right foot, which is firmly planted. The left heel may leave the ground slightly, yet some pros, including myself, keep that left foot planted.

Now you're at the top of your backswing. A pause, ever so slight, is in order here. This is to allow your body the full benefit of getting everything into that downswing. On the downswing your weight flows smoothly to the left side, and the left foot (if you lift your heel) goes back to its original position. As you come down through the swing, your right foot rolls over to the inside and the heel might start to lift slightly just before impact.

Good balance throughout the swing flows from proper footwork, rhythm, timing, and making the good turn. By turn I don't mean swaying "off the ball" or away from the target. I don't mean lunging at the ball on the downswing. Rhythm and timing come through natural ability and through practice. Every time you swing a golf club properly you are doing much to groove your swing so that you'll be able to call on it at any time and know it won't fail you.

Let's go back a bit to the waggle. Each time you waggle the club back, your right elbow should hit the front part of your right hip, just about where your watch pocket should be. Then the left elbow comes out slightly, the lower part of the arm from the elbow down rotates, and the left hand moves away from the target. As the hands move back to the ball on the forward waggle, the left hand moves slightly forward past the ball and toward the target. During the waggle the upper part of the arms remains against the sides of the chest. As we said before, there definitely should *not* be a turn of the shoulders during the waggle.

A word of caution! DON'T GROOVE YOUR WAGGLE. This is impossible since the various lies you come across make it impossible to waggle the same way each time. Say you're playing a seven iron and want to hit a soft, feathery shot to a green. In this case your waggle will be slower and somewhat soft. This is the tempo you'll also be using on the stroke. If you want to hit a long shot with a low trajectory, your waggle now will be brisk and much speedier. And you'll swing that way. In other words, your waggle fits the tempo of your swing.

There is one point that should be emphasized here: THE DIFFERENCE BETWEEN THE WAGGLE AND THE BACKSWING IS THAT DURING THE WAGGLE YOUR SHOULDERS DO NOT MOVE! Right at the beginning of the backswing, however, your shoulders start that slow turn. The backswing is initiated by the simultaneous movement of the hands, arms, and shoulders. Getting the shoulders into action does *not* alter the pattern of your waggle. By

THE WAGGLE
DO NOT
MOVE YOUR SHOULDERS
DURING THE WAGGLE
DO
KEEP THE UPPER ARMS
AGAINST THE SIDES OF
YOUR CHEST

increasing the the arc of your waggle, you just naturally bring your shoulders into play.

On the backswing the movement goes like this: HANDS, ARMS, HIPS, AND THEN SHOULDERS. On the downswing the order is reversed: hips, shoulders, arms, and hands. The hands start the clubhead back just before the arms come into it and a split second before the shoulders begin their turn. As the golfer develops a grooved swing through much practice, the hands, arms, and shoulders will instinctively move into the right position at every point in the take-away and backswing and then into the downswing. This is a unified action.

On the backswing the hips are always ahead of the shoulders as they turn. As the hips begin to turn, they pull the left leg in and to the right. You want to turn your shoulders as far as they'll go *without moving your head.* When you reach your maximum turn, your back should face squarely toward the target. Of course, the more shoulder turn, the more power you generate. Most golfers think they make the full shoulder turn, but the truth is, FEW AMATEUR PLAYERS REALLY COMPLETE THE FULL SHOULDER TURN! They stop turning about halfway around, and then, in order to get the clubhead all the way back, they'll break the left arm.

Remember, a golfer *cannot* have control of his club or start into his downswing with any power unless his left arm is straight to start with. When you bend your left arm, you actually perform a half swing and forfeit half of your potential power. Moreover, you just naturally make many other movements which are exhausting and do nothing whatever in polishing your swing.

A good way to check yourself out on this full shoulder turn is WHEN YOU FINISH YOUR BACKSWING, YOUR CHIN SHOULD BE AGAINST THE TOP OF YOUR LEFT SHOULDER! In most cases it's about an inch from the end of your shoulder.

Turning the hips too soon is another common error. This immediately destroys your chance of having the power an integrated swing gives you. As you begin your backswing, restrain your hips from moving until the shoulders pull them into their turn.

Some pros advocate a big hip turn. I disagree since I want tension on the midsection of my body. Tension is the key to the whole downswing. The downswing is initiated by turning the hips back to the left. Then you have all this tension stored up and ready to trigger when you begin the downswing. The tension which makes your shoulders pull your hips automatically helps you pull down into the ball. It is this increased tension that unwinds the upper part of your body. It then unwinds the shoulders, arms, and hands in the correct order. This tension also helps make your swing almost automatic.

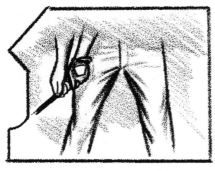

THE BACKSWING

IT'S ONE . . .
THE HANDS START IT ALL

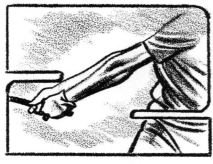

. . . TWO . . .
THEN THE ARMS TAKE OVER

. . . THREE . . .
THE HIPS FOLLOW

. . . AND FOUR
AND THE SHOULDERS COMPLETE
THE BACKSWING

Maximum tension in the muscles between the hips and the shoulders produces maximum speed. The tighter the tension, the faster your upper body will unwind and transfer its speed to the hands. This gives the upper part of the body a running start. This is the speed which eventually produces clubhead speed, which in turn gives you that feeling of power. If your hips were turned as much as your shoulders, there'd be no tightening of the muscles at all and therefore no clubhead speed.

Now for the legs. When the hips enter the backswing, as they turn, this pulls in the left leg. The left knee breaks into the right, the left foot rolls to the right on the inside of the sole, and what weight is left is on the inside ball of the foot.

I'm not advocating it, but *if* you raise your left heel (which I have explained before is not my cup of tea), make it ever so slight. If you bring your left heel too far off the ground, this will immediately throw you into a faulty balance from which you *cannot* recover.

Let the body and legs move your feet. As far as the right leg is concerned, throughout the backswing it should remain in the same position it was at address. When you have a stable right leg and the right knee is pointed in slightly, it prevents the leg from sagging and swaying out to the right and carrying the body along with it.

That just about takes care of the first part of the swing. In the next chapter we're going to get into the crux of the whole thing —hitting the golf ball. This includes the downswing and is the culmination of all we've learned so far: the grip, stance, takeaway, backswing. And what a thrill it is when you have everything in the right perspective to bang one down the middle of the fairway. You're loose and easy and rhythmic, and you know what you can do each time you line up a shot. So work on the past lessons and get sharp. We're really getting into it now. . . .

6 THE DOWNSWING

The secret of long hitting is to accelerate the club-head speed on the downswing gradually and delay uncocking the wrists until the hands pass the belt line.

Much has been said about the first movement on the down-swing. Some would have you turning your hips back to the left. Others would have you pull downward with the left hand and arm. And there are those who would have you start with the shift of weight.

One thing about it, you can't think of all these things at once. This has to be a continuing action with all factors working as one —the hips, the arms, the hand, the shoulders. Speaking of shoulders, there's a natural tendency for the right shoulder to be too high when you come through the swing. This causes the clubhead to make contact on top of the ball. We certainly don't want this. However, we'll get into the subject of the shoulders later.

Before we start the downward part of the swing, it would be a good idea to study the plane of it. As the golfer addresses the ball, he creates the plane of his backswing. If the player rotates his shoulders on an even keel on the backswing, he supposedly wants to keep the same plane on his downswing. However, this isn't so. As you come down, the plane is less steep and quite different from the backswing. The golfer gets this new plane without even thinking about it. This occurs when he turns his hips back to the left as he starts the downswing. This moves his body to the left, and he automatically brings his shoulders into a different position.

Now, back to the shoulders. As we said before, the average golfer has a tendency to hold his right shoulder too high. One reason for this is that the right-handed golfer has an inherent left-side weakness and may put the right side into the swing too soon or use a pushing or throwing motion. As a result, the wrists uncock too soon—at the top of the backswing—and this throws the right elbow out too far, causing an outside-in swing.

Centrifugal force makes it a natural tendency to come over the top, which causes a raising of the head too soon. Looking up too soon causes the head to turn away too quickly. Probably the best way to regulate the shoulders is to think of them as a pendulum on a grandfather clock. The shoulders should preferably tilt vertically, with the right shoulder passing under the chin at impact and follow-through.

Tall players find it easier to tilt their shoulders vertically. However, short golfers can assure that their right shoulder stays low by pulling the club down with the left arm and at the same time tucking in the right elbow close to the body. This is ideally the only way to cause the perfect swing—inside-out.

We're finally ready to hit the ball—and remember: THE HIPS INITIATE THE DOWNSWING. They are the pivotal element in the chain action. Starting the hips first *makes* the downswing. It generates early speed; it transfers the weight from the right to the left foot; it takes the hips out of the way and gives the arms plenty of room; it puts you in a strong hitting position where the big muscles in the back, arms, and shoulders are properly delayed so they can produce the maximum force at point of impact.

To begin the downswing, turn your hips back to the left, and remember, there must be enough lateral movement to transfer the weight to the left foot. As I said before, the path that the hips take on the downswing isn't the same as the one they traveled on the backswing. The arc on the downswing will be slightly flatter.

HIPS INITIATE THE DOWNSWING

SHOULDERS SHOULD ACT
LIKE THE TOP OF A PENDULUM

THE HANDS SHOULD UNCOCK AT IMPACT

THE IRONS FROM THE FRONT

THE WOODS FROM THE BACK

This turning of the hips is activated by several sets of muscles that work together—the contracted muscles of the left hip and the muscles along the inside of the left thigh begin to spin the left hip to the left. At the same time, the muscles of the right hip and the right thigh start to move the right hip forward. These muscles have been stretched taut by retarding the hips but rotating the shoulders fully around on the backswing. The greater the tension, the faster you can move the hips. The faster the hips, the more powerful the swing.

The movement of the hips starts a chain reaction. As you begin your downward swing, the left leg starts turning toward the target. Also, the left knee, naturally, bends toward the target. Now the weight begins to flow to the left leg. The right knee breaks in, boosting the mounting velocity of the swing.

Here is what is happening at this point:

The cohesive movement of the body, legs, and arms toward the target multiplies the golfer's power some fifteen times over. In the chain action of the swing the shoulders and upper part of the body conduct this multiplying power into the arms and the arms multiply it again to the hands and the hands transfer this generating power to the club. At point of impact the clubhead is traveling at an enormous rate of speed. And, as we have discussed before, the faster the clubhead speed, the greater the distance of your shot.

Most poor golfers destroy this entire concept by starting their swings with the hands. By beginning with the hands, they kill their chances for good shots by checking the rotation of the hips, and this forces the body outside the proper plane. The golfer is committed to bring the club from the outside in, and he invariably slices the ball. And if he doesn't slice, he'll pull the ball to the left as he tries to compensate for his original error of not starting his downswing with the hips.

To put it more strongly:THE 15-HANDICAPPER SHOULD KEEP ANY CONSCIOUS HAND ACTION OUT OF HIS SWING. THE PERFECT SWING IS FOUNDED ON CHAIN ACTION, AND THE USE OF THE HANDS, KNOWINGLY, WILL DESTROY THIS ACTION.

At this point you may ask: What *do* the hands do? Actually, they do nothing active until after the arms have moved to a position just above hip level. Up to this point, the arms have been carried along by the hip movements. As the hands move to just above hip level, they are loaded with power and ready to pick up the tremendous load of energy stored in your body. Now the hands take over in guiding the clubhead to point of impact.

Of course, all this happens in one unbroken thrust—hips, arms, and hands—ending with the follow-through. The follow-through is just a correct extension of the correct swing. Let's examine the follow-through. At impact point the left side is solid—straight left arm, left leg, and left foot planted. The right arm, which was tucked neatly in close to the body as the swing got down to hip level, expends its power just beyond impact and begins to straighten out. The right foot, at impact, is dug in and pointed at right angles to the target, but after impact the right heel will raise as the full weight of the body is transferred entirely to the left side.

Although the left hand is the power hand, you're supposed to hit the ball with full power with both hands. At impact the back of the left hand faces toward the target and the wristbone is definitely raised and, as the ball is hit, nearer to the target than any other part of the hand. When the left wrist is in this position, there is no danger of the right hand overpowering the left and twisting the club over. Every pro has his wrist in this supinating position at impact. When his club comes into the ball, he starts to pronate the left wrist—turns it so the palm will face downward.

Keeping the wrist in a supinating position at impact gives the golfer more distance and accuracy. In this way he hits the ball cleanly *before* the club takes turf. Another thing, supination places the hands a little ahead of the clubhead at impact, and you hit the ball in a direct line. In other words, it takes some loft off the shot.

Another thing that should be emphasized: Supination enables you to get maximum grip and backspin on the ball. This is the explanation of one of the most amazing shots in the game today —the low-flying wedge that looks as if it were skulled but that bites when it lands and then spins itself out close to where it landed.

When you're playing short shots—chips, pitches, and trap shots —the hands should function the same as on a full swing. With the exception of the trap shot, remember, you always hit the ball first and the turf second. Hit the ball on the downswing and the club face will supply the loft.

There are a couple of misconceptions at point of impact that I'll try to clear up for you. Most golfers think that at impact both arms should be perfectly straight. Not so—the left arm is straight but the right is slightly bent. On the downswing the right arm gradually straightens out as it comes into the ball, but it isn't until the clubhead is about two feet past the point where you have hit the ball that the right arm is fully extended. In fact, it is at this point that *both* the right and left arms are perfectly straight. After this, the left arm begins to fold in at the elbow and the right arm remains straight right on through the complete swing.

Another point: It is just beyond the point of impact that the clubhead reaches its full velocity, *not* at point of impact. This speed is what carries the player right on around to that high

finish. At the completion of his swing the golfer's belt buckle should point directly at the target. The hips lead the shoulders all the way on the downswing, and the shoulders finally catch up with the hips at the completion of the swing.

As for the legs: On a good swing, when the player's hands are approaching the hip level on the downswing, his hips have reached the point in their turn when they have begun to open on their way to facing the target. The two legs respond to the hips, the right leg breaking in at the knee, while the straight left leg takes on the full weight of the body.

If the swing has been properly executed, a golfer will have his hands high and be able to hold this position for three or four seconds. If he's off balance and falling forward or backward, he'd better do some checking. I feel I swing with about 85 per cent of my power. If you swing with 100 per cent, your shot may stray. While I do *not* like a lazy swing, I feel that I have more control with about an 85 per cent effort.

So now that you've got the grip, the stance, the take-away, the backswing, and the downswing, it's time for some action. But before that we'll do some reviewing. In the next chapter we'll go over everything we have covered to date. After all, the basics are the most important part of golf.

7 REVIEW OF THE BASICS

Golf, like any other endeavor, changes with the times. As we get older and wiser, we bring in new things and discard the old. As I said before, this book is a culmination of my knowledge as a golfer which spans some twenty-five years. Each year I learned something new, something that improved my game. In another ten years there'll be other changes, but the preceding chapters reflect my game as of the present. And the fundamentals of the game, along with dedicated practice, are what makes any golfer. I am firmly convinced that all that is required to play good golf is execution of a small number of fundamental moves.

So let's review the first thing we got into, the grip:

Left hand—Place the club so that the shaft is pressed up under the heel of the hand. The shaft should also lie across the joint of the forefinger. The pressure points are the last three fingers and the heel pad. The V should be pointing at the right eye.

Right hand—This is a finger grip all the way. The shaft should run across the top joint of the fingers but below the palm. The two middle fingers apply most of the pressure. To prove what these three fingers will do, practice with the thumb and forefinger off the shaft. The V on the right hand should point at the chin.

Both hands—Both hands should work together as one. The little finger of the right hand should lock into the groove between the forefinger and big finger of the left hand. The left thumb should fit perfectly into the cup of the right palm.

Now let's go into the stance:

There is just one basic stance: the right foot is at right angles to the target; the left foot is pointed out about a quarter of a turn and slightly behind the right. With a driver, the feet should be no wider than the width of the shoulders. The stance then narrows for the shorter clubs until you get down to the wedge, when the feet will be six inches closer together. That's right, from the driver to the nine iron, the distance should have narrowed by six inches. It is important to keep the elbows and arms as close together as possible. The knees should point in. When you bend the knees, the upper part of the body remains erect. The right elbow should point right at the right hip. The left elbow should point at the left hip. The correct stance will govern the right amount of hip turn.

The take-away:

When you waggle the club, make sure that the hands move together and that the waggle motion is the same as you're going to use in your swing. Hands, arms, and shoulders start the club back in one easy motion. When the shoulders turn, they automatically turn the hips. The correct tension in the muscles is created by the hip turn. Remember, this is a turn, not a sway.

The downswing:

The turning of the hips back to the left starts the downswing. The big point in the downswing is that the hips initiate the movement, not the arms, hands, or shoulders. In the chain action of the downswing, the turning of the hips to the left releases the body, legs, and arms in one movement. As the golfer enters the swing, each component part of the body contributes to the increasing speed and power of the swing. The shoulders and upper part of the body conduct the power into the arms, the arms multiply it again and pass it on to the hands. Then the hands increase it again to the clubhead. The clubhead is going at a tremendous rate of speed at the impact point. Just before impact the left wrist begins to supinate and the left wristbone is raised and faces directly toward the target.

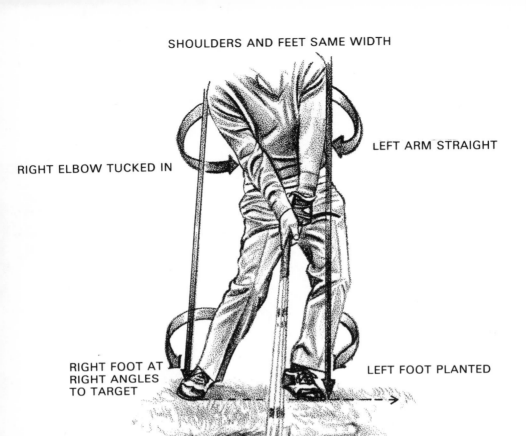

SHOULDERS AND FEET SAME WIDTH

LEFT ARM STRAIGHT

RIGHT ELBOW TUCKED IN

RIGHT FOOT AT
RIGHT ANGLES
TO TARGET

LEFT FOOT PLANTED

This is the complete swing stripped down to the bare basics. This is all the player needs to know to develop a correct grooved swing that will stay with him under all conditions. The golfer whose swing is founded on this chain action is bound to have timing. The swing has arranged the timing for him. The golfer has to learn only one swing. He uses this swing for every shot in the book. The ball should be played farther forward on the long shots. When you narrow the width of the stance, you quite naturally move the right foot progressively closer to the left foot and toward the ball.

Whether you're playing a driver, middle iron, or short iron, you make no variation in your swing. The shorter the shaft, the closer the player must stand to the ball. A suggestion: Make a small modification when you're playing clubs from the seven iron down to the wedge ... get the hips out of the way *before* you begin your stroke. You do this by setting the right foot a bit closer to the ball at the point of address. When you play the short clubs this way, you have the feeling that you're taking a full swing; actually, you're not.

That's it in a nutshell, as they say in squirrel land. Now we're ready for the practice tee. In the next few chapters we'll be going up the ladder, so to speak, from the wedge to the driver. Also, we'll be touching on the odd shots—sand, rough, uphill and downhill lies—or anything pertaining to the great game of golf. Remember, I promised to take from ten to fifteen shots off your game.

8 CHIPPING

Editor's note: Chi Chi practices his short game so much that he says: "I feel as though I were on the green when I'm within fifty yards of the cup. No one ever has as much luck around the greens as one who practices a lot."

The chip shot is that delicate operation near the green where, with a little practice, you can get up and in with a maximum of two strokes. This is the shot in which most amateurs can be as good as the best with a little concentration and, of course, practice. To express it as simply as possible, it's like tossing a ball underhand to a designated spot.

Now, I'm talking about the chip, *not* the pitch shot. There's a definite difference between the two. A chip has a lower trajectory because you're using, in most cases, a less lofted club. The player hitting the chip wants to land on the green and run the ball to-

CHIPPING IS LIKE TOSSING A BALL UNDERHAND
TO A DESIGNATED SPOT ON THE GREEN

ward the hole. And there is *no backspin!* Another point—with the chip your weight should be 90 per cent on your left side at all times.

You can pick out a high-handicapper right away if he plays all his chips with a nine iron or wedge. There is no way you can use a lofted club time and again on the chip shot. The reason for this is that you'll run into different lies around the green. You might be on the frog hair where the grass is slightly higher than the green. Or you might be a little farther back in the tall grass where a lofted club would be the right club to use. Or the green might be tilted toward you or, in another case, away from you. Or the green could be fast or slow. Also, there could be an obstacle, such as a low tree or a trap between your ball and the cup. There are so many variables here that you just can't say, "I'm going to use a nine iron," every time you approach one of these shots.

First of all, the chip swing is all arms and hands. It's almost like putting. And this may shock you, but the best club in your bag for a chip *is* your putter. Of course, this is only when you're very near the green, say on the frog hair. This brings up another problem. Most amateurs will hit the ball too hard when putting off the frog hair. Again, you have to know the thickness of the grass, the roll of the green, the bent of the grass. And the only way you'll get to know just how hard to hit the ball is to practice on the practice tee. The grass on the tee will invariably be the same as on the entire course. So a few chip shots around the practice tee or practice green will give you the feel of whatever club you're going to use.

Now, say you're about 30 feet off the putting surface; the pin is 40 feet farther and the green is level. In this situation I use my seven iron. This allows me to get the ball up and over the fairway grass, and when it lands on the green it will roll toward the cup.

The club should be brought back low to the ground with the arms and hands. You choke up on the club to where it feels comfortable. The backswing is no higher than your hands. The left hand should lead the clubhead down and through the shot. There should be *no wrist* in this short shot; it's *all arms.*

A word or two of warning on this shot—you can get into trouble with it. As I said before, this *is not* a wrist shot. If you use your wrists on the take-away and backswing, you'll lift the club too fast, and this causes a scooping action. The wrist break also can cause sculling—hitting on top of the ball. Also, you've heard of shanking. Well, this is the shot where most of the shanks are made. So remember, it's strictly an arm shot.

A good rule to follow on the chip shot is, "One-third by air and two-thirds by land." In other words, when you're chipping it's usually better to get the ball on the putting surface as soon as

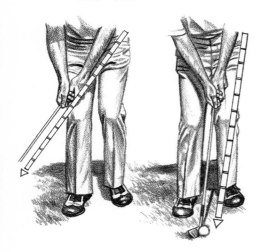 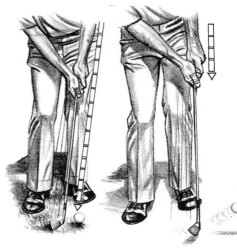

possible and let the ball roll the rest of the way, as if it were a putt.

Also, the chip shot is a relaxed rhythmical thing, *but* it also has to be a firm shot. And, being a feel shot, it takes a lot of practice. Since it requires little space, you can practice in your own back yard. For instance, I get a kick out of drawing a three-foot circle in my yard and then seeing how many shots, percentage-wise, I can get inside the circle. I'll vary the distance from time to time so I'll be able to get the true feel of the various clubs I use on the chip shot.

Most successful golfers "spot chip," much as the pro bowlers "spot bowl." You pick out a spot on the green where you want your ball to land. Then you take a few practice swings to get the feel, or the force, with which you want to hit the ball. Then you address the ball, recheck your spot, and go into the shot. You'll be surprised how little practice it takes to find that you can put the ball on the spot almost every time.

Also, the club should hit the ball first, then the ground, just as on your other shots. This gives you a feeling of crispness at the point of impact. Another thing—keep your hands ahead of the clubhead at all times until the ball is on its way.

You should use an open stance on the chip shot. I always align myself so that I play the ball off my right toe. You'll find this way of aligning yourself simplifies hitting your spot on the green each time.

Now, we've had one example of the chip shot—the one where the ball was off the green by 30 feet and the green was level and we used a seven iron. Here's another situation: Again you're off the green by 30 feet and the green tilts toward you. This means you'll have to hit the ball a little harder and get more roll. So I usually pick out a five iron. This club is less lofted and consequently the ball will roll farther after hitting the spot you've picked out.

Here's another example: Once more you're 30 feet from the green, only this time the pin is only 6 feet from the edge of your side of the green. You'll have to hit this shot higher so you'll have some bite on it. A wedge is your club this time. Okay, so you'll hold the wedge with the same grip you used previously with the seven and five irons. Since you'll want the ball to get into the air quicker and get down faster, you'll play the wedge open. You have the same grip on this club as on the others—you've shortened your grip, and your left arm is guiding the club down and through the ball. With the putting stroke—as before—the ball will flip into the air for the short distance and land softly on the green. The soft landing will allow for the short roll to the hole.

Another bit of battle-tested advice to keep you from shanking: As in every shot in your bag, you have to keep the head almost perfectly still. Any sway will immediately throw off the shot so you won't know where it's going. Since a sway will throw your hands much ahead of the ball at point of impact, the result is the dreaded shank that is the bane of all amateurs. And you must keep the elbows rigid and six to eight inches apart at all times.

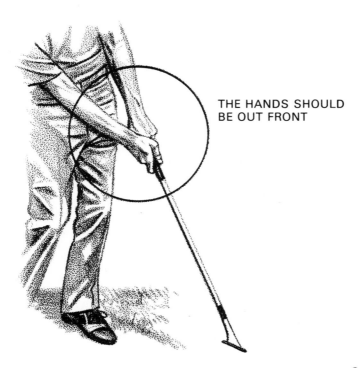

THE HANDS SHOULD
BE OUT FRONT

Let's put you in another situation: This time the ball is nestled in the thick grass just off the frog hair. This means you want to get the ball up and out of there as quickly as possible, so again you must turn to the wedge. This chip shot is more like a chop. And as in previous chips, you hit down into the ball and take grass and turf after the blow. However, this time you're going to have to use the wrists. The wrists give you more power, which you'll need to pull the club through the high grass.

There's a hole at the Masters Tournament where the green tilts away from the approaching golfer. This hole has ruined more golf scores at Augusta than any other on the course. You simply can't hold a shot with any degree of consistency. It's a par four with a pond at the back of the green. So I try to hit my second shot short where I can use a wedge chip to the hole. Playing the hole this way assures me of getting my par, and if I happen to chip it in I've got a birdie—something that happens to too few of the touring players on this hole.

I said earlier in the chapter that the putter is the best club in your bag for the chip shot. This is because there is less movement with the putter and you have more control over it than over any of your other clubs. And there are times when it's advisable to come out of the sand with your putter. Of course, you won't use your putter if there is an overhang on the edge of the trap. But we'll get to the sand shots in a later chapter.

In summation of the chip shot: Choose the club that the situation demands. Use *only* the arms and hands except when you're in the high grass. Keep your swing relaxed and rhythmical. Keep your feet close together and play the ball off your right toe. On most shots you'll be using a seven iron, or even a five, where you get some roll. If at all possible use the putter. Choke the club—in other words, shorten up on the grip. Keep your hands ahead of the ball at all times until the clubhead makes contact. The backswing should never be more than hands high. Hit down and through the ball before taking any turf. Don't lift the club too fast, as this will cause sculling or shanking. "Spot chipping" is a tried and true practice. Above all, chipping is a delicate operation and takes plenty of practice. So draw that circle in your back yard and go at it. You'll find success is closer than you think. The simple explanation: The chip shot is like tossing the ball underhanded to a given spot.

9 PITCHING

Unlike the lower trajectory of the chip shot, the pitch shot is longer, you use a more lofted club, it's a higher shot that floats to the green, you use the wrists, and in most cases you hit the ball so as to get backspin. But, as in the chip, you use an open stance, you have your feet in almost the same position, according to distance, and the backswing is higher—to the waist, in this case.

As we said earlier, the pitch shot is longer—up to 75 yards. And in most cases you'll be using a wedge. The wedge, being the highest lofted club in the bag, naturally gives you a floating shot—high and feathery. And this action, naturally, gives you a bite, or backspin, on the shot.

In the chip shot you're hitting the ball off your right toe with an open stance. In the pitch shot you close the clubface slightly, and instead of having your weight about 90 per cent on your left foot, you hit from a more balanced stance. Your hands are still ahead of the ball but not as much as with the chip.

Of course, there are a couple of variations of the pitch. They are known as the cut shot and the punch shot. The punch shot is used mostly in a cross wind or directly into the wind. Since the trajectory should be lower, you don't open your stance as much as on the normal pitch shot. Play the ball a little farther back, with your hands ahead of the ball at point of address. Use the waist-high backswing, hit the ball first, and then take turf just after impact. The follow-through is restricted.

The cut-pitch shot is just the opposite. This is used when the wind is at your back, or when you have a bunker to clear, or when you have to hit over a high obstacle such as a tree. Your most important aspect of the cut shot is that you must stop the ball quickly.

The ball is played off the left heel with the open stance. Your hands are even with the ball at point of address. You swing back with your hands and arms and flatten out the swing arc at point of impact. Again, you hit the ball first and take turf second. You also finish with the hands high.

A note of caution: The cut shot can be hit only when the ball is sitting up high. It's certainly not the type of shot you can hit off a hard surface or from a tight lie, since the sole of the clubhead

THE HIGH FLOATER

THE RUN-IN SHOT

WHEN YOU LINE UP LIKE THIS,

YOU GET THIS **(THE SHANK)**

BUT BY LOWERING THE
RIGHT SHOULDER AND
KEEPING THE ARMS STRAIGHT,

RESULTS ARE   SWEET SHOTS!

will bounce into the ball and the result will be a sculled or topped shot.

As in the chip shot, accuracy is of the utmost importance. You play the ball slightly toward the right heel with the open stance. This open stance restricts my full shoulder and hip turn, which makes it a must to take a shorter backswing and assures me of a more accurate shot. Remember, you measure accurate drives in yards and accurate short irons in feet.

A good rhythmic and unhurried swing is important with the pitch shot. Of course, good tempo is important for all the clubs in your bag. With this shot I try not to force the hitting action but rather just to swing through and throw my arms out toward the target.

Back to accuracy: Approach the ball from the rear so as to line it up with the green. Set the clubhead down behind the ball so it will be in line with the green in order to establish the ball line. Then line up the feet for the shot, maintaining the same ball line with the clubhead in relation to the ball.

Now you're set up for the shot. The left shoulder moves back as you slowly go into your take-away. You continue your backswing until it reaches your waist. You're at the top of your backswing when your hips begin their turn into the ball. The wrists remain almost static, depending on the need for loft in the shot. If you're going over an obstacle, such as a tree, you'll have to use more wrists to get more lift into your swing. As has been mentioned, the delayed uncocking of the wrists gives you more power and consequently more lift to your swing. You're now coming into the ball, and you must be sure that you hit the ball first and then the turf. Your hands, arms, and shoulders finish high.

As we said in the previous chapter, one of the banes of the amateur is shanking of the chip and pitch shots. One of the causes of shanking is the straightening of the body in the pelvic region during the backswing, which tends to cause a flattening of the swing. This, in turn, throws the clubhead out of its proper plane, and the neck of the club hits the ball.

Now to correct this common happening, the base of the neck should *not move* forward or backward, or up or down, during the entire swing and follow-through. The player should address the ball by bending slightly from the waist with the knees slightly flexed. Neither the knees nor the back should straighten during the take-away or backswing.

Another common ailment that causes shanking is looping. Looping happens when the golfer moves his head and shoulders on the backswing forward and to the left so they are more over the ball on the downswing. This also moves his hands and club outside their normal position at the top of the backswing so that they, too, are more over the ball. This forces the clubhead to return to the ball from the outside, increasing the chances for the ball again to be hit on the neck of the clubhead instead of on the clubhead itself.

How can this problem be corrected? Looping will disappear if the player takes a slightly fuller turn with his hips and shoulders on the backswing, being careful at the same time *not* to flatten the swing. The player should feel that his chin remains pointed at the ball throughout the downswing and until after the impact point.

Standing too far from the ball also is a major cause of shanking. After a golfer hits a shank shot, he tends to stand farther away on his next pitch shot. Of course, this just flattens out his swing more and more, and a flat swing is a sure shot into the ways of the shank.

To correct this, stand closer to the ball and accentuate tilting and turning the shoulders. Lowering the left shoulder and raising the right shoulder on the backswing results in a downswing that follows a more upright plane.

Another big problem in the pitch shot is "sclaffing," or hitting the fat shot. This is caused by hitting the ground before you hit the ball. This causes the clubhead to slow down a second before impact, and this produces poor contact with the ball as grass and dirt come between the clubhead and the ball.

TO CURE THE FAT SHOT . . . LEAN YOUR HEAD AGAINST A WALL AND SWING WITHOUT A CLUB. AFTER YOU GET THE FEELING OF NOT DUCKING YOUR HEAD, REPEAT THIS ACTION *WITH* A CLUB BUT *WITHOUT* THE WALL

One of the main causes of the fat shot is crouching at point of address. The player positions himself so that his suspension point (the back of his neck) is closer to the ball than the distance formed by the length of his arms and the part of the club below his hands. This crouching causes a bent elbow at address. Obviously, this incorrect position will carry through his backswing and downswing, and the clubhead will be lower at impact than it was during address. The clubhead will hit the dirt and your shot will finish far short of the target.

THE SHORT SHOT SHIFT
WEIGHT TRANSFER FROM LEFT TO RIGHT IS A MAJOR CONCERN
FOR WEEKENDERS. TO GET THE FEEL, SWING A LOFTED CLUB IN A
SHORT PENDULUM-LIKE ARC. START SLOWLY AND INCREASE
THE SWING ARC UNTIL YOU ARE SWINGING FULL TILT.

To correct this fault, all you do is shorten the swing radius or raise the suspension point. To shorten the radius you simply shorten your grip, or choke up, on the club. Of course, you'll lose distance in this operation. The other way to correct the sclaff (raising the suspension point) will widen your swing arc by causing you to extend your arms at address point. You raise the suspension point merely by addressing the ball from a more upright position.

There's another thing to consider in this suspension point. As we covered in a previous chapter, your arc is wider on the downswing than it was in the backswing. So there's a chance that your arc will change on the downswing even after raising your suspension point at address. The obvious answer to this is to keep your head from ducking. One way to work on this part of your game would be to lean your head against a wall or tree and swing *without* a club. This will give you an idea of what it feels like to swing without lowering the head. Then duplicate this feeling without the wall or tree but *with a club.*

Another reason for sclaffing is improperly fitted clubs that are too flexible. Too whippy a club shaft can produce fat shots even though your swing is correct. In this case, the bending shaft as it comes through the downswing causes the clubhead to drag along the ground at point of impact. This is especially true of a strong player with a forceful swing. A strong golfer sacrifices control if he uses too whippy a shaft, while the weak swinger may lose clubhead speed by using too stiff a shaft.

A while back I noted that to hit the ideal feathery pitch shot to the green your ball must be sitting up. So what happens if you find yourself in heavy grass? You really have to have an iron grip on the club to hit a heavy-grass shot. Play the ball in the middle of your feet and move the clubhead slowly but positively through the heavy grass. This is true on both the backswing and the downswing. But first you have to lift the clubhead rather than take it back on a low level. Then you more or less chop down on the ball. Hitting down on the ball with a sharp angle of descent allows the clubhead to contact the ball before speed is slowed by the intervening grass.

What happens if your ball is on a hard surface? Well, in this case you keep your weight well to the left and avoid taking a divot. The ball must come off the hard surface at a tremendous rate of speed. With your weight forward, your hands will be well ahead of the ball and the clubface will be tipped forward at contact, which will diminish the club's normal loft. This makes the flight of the ball low, so use the next higher club—if it's a normal seven-iron shot, use an eight iron.

How about the pitch shot off soggy turf? This requires greater

balance than in most shots, so you have to be sure you're anchored securely before you go into the swing, as in the sand shot. The idea on this shot is to clip the ball off the grass without taking much of a divot. To help assure a clean stroke at impact, play the ball well forward—off the left foot—and level your swing arc at point of impact.

Rounding up the ingredients of the pitch shot: Play the ball more toward the middle of the feet with the feet not more than twelve inches apart. Use the open stance in most cases. As with the chip shot, make a study of the grass before you start your round. Never take your club above the waist on the backswing, except when you're in deep grass. Be slow and deliberate, so the swing will be rhythmic and smooth. Use very little wrist action except out of the tall grass or when you have to go over a tree. Also, in these two exceptions play the ball more to the center of your feet. If you have to hit off a hard surface, play the ball in front with the hands well forward and take no divot. Since the pitch shot is a delicate one, it requires a lot of practice. So get out there in the back yard, draw a circle, and go to work. We're still going to take those ten to fifteen strokes off your game before all this is over.

10 THE FINESSE CLUBS (SEVEN, EIGHT, NINE, AND WEDGE)

As in pitching and chipping, the seven, eight, and nine irons, and the wedge are very important in lowering a score. And use of these clubs is just an extension of the shorter game. You can use these clubs from 100 yards in, depending on how far you hit the ball.

A popular shot the pros use is the run-up shot. This shot can be played with either the seven, eight, or nine iron—of course, depending on the wind and the terrain. On this shot you want to hit in front of the green, bounce on, and then let 'er roll toward the cup. This shot is especially good when greens are hard and won't hold. And when the wind is against you.

Let's say you're 90 yards from the green and feel you should hit a run-up shot. I'd pick the seven iron in this case, but, of course, this again is up to the individual. The seven, in my case, will carry the ball over any rough fairway and still give a considerable bounce and roll.

When I'm planning a shot like this, I like to picture the ball landing in a certain spot in front of the green. Your stance for run-up shots should be fairly narrow, with the feet equidistant from the intended flight of the ball. The ball is played toward the center of the stance, with the hands well forward. Of course, the shorter the shot the more open your stance. This is for accuracy. As there should be as little backspin as possible, don't beat down on the ball but rather level out the swing at the impact point and take only a small divot. And, keep the ball low.

Although the run-up shot is useful in the wind and on hard greens, the usual procedure for normal shots like this is to use a nine iron and float the ball toward the smoother surface of the green.

Getting back to a point I just made: hitting down on the ball. The more directly you hit down on the ball with a short iron, the more backspin you'll apply. This produces a high-rising shot that just won't do against the wind. But to avoid a severe up-and-down clubhead path, I move the clubhead away and low to the ground on my take-away with my left arm fully extended. There definitely is *no wrist break* early. On these shots the backswing need not be as long as normal—say about three-quarters of the usual shot. The low, wide take-away will cause the clubhead to follow through on a fairly flat or level arc to the point of impact. This reduces backspin and helps keep the ball low. And as in chipping, be sure to keep about 90 per cent of your weight on the left foot.

The biggest fault the amateur has with these lofted clubs is that he's afraid he won't get enough into his swing. Most high handicappers try to help the ball into the air with all kinds of body maneuvers. The most prevalent is breaking the wrists forward at the impact point. If you will just stand there and sort of flick at the ball with your hands and wrists, you'll find these clubs are very easy to use.

It's always difficult for the novice to believe that with the short swing he'll be able to get any distance. He therefore lunges at the ball, and the results are sclaffing (hitting behind the ball), shanking, and topping. Again, the same rule applies to these clubs as applied when hitting the pitch or the chip shots: Pick out a place in front of the green and concentrate on hitting that spot. Forget about where the ball is going to end up and practice hitting that one spot. And, as always, be relaxed and comfortable.

I gave you a previous example of hitting toward a hard green or into the wind with the run-in shot. But say the green is soft and you know you're not going to get much of a roll. Naturally, you have to think of a high, floating shot that will land as close to the pin as possible. I know a lot of the pros say they play all shots for the center of the green, but when the green is soft you can throw the ball right at the pin. In this case you use the highest lofted club you feel you can reach, play the ball midway in the stance, and come *down* into the shot. This, of course, puts the needed backspin on the ball.

Something just occurred to me that should be valuable to the novice. To avoid scooping the ball with these irons, I always keep my hands ahead of the clubhead. In this way I use my left hand as the guide. I like to feel that my left hand pushes the clubhead back and pulls it through the shot. I never feel that I'm scooping the ball into the air with my right hand. I let the loft of the clubface take care of that.

Another thing which we discussed in the chapter on the grip was holding the club lightly. This is especially important with the seven, eight, nine, and wedge. The example I gave: Pretend you're holding a little bird and don't want it to get away. This light but firm hold on the club produces the desired effect without wearing you out.

Now, here are a few tips I'm going to give you so you'll know how to play the greens on courses with which you are not familiar:

1. Extra large greens normally look closer than what they are. When you come to a big green, be sure *not* to underclub yourself.

With small greens it's just the opposite. They seem farther away than they are, so don't overclub in approaching them.

2. Varying pin positions on extra-large greens can call for as much as four clubs' difference from front to back. Be sure to check with your caddie as to pin placements before hitting your approach shot.

3. When there's a swale or dip in the terrain in front of the green, the shot will seem much shorter than it actually is. Again check with your caddie for any funny-looking breaks in the fairway.

4. When the green is below your approach position, the shot will take less club than you think. Of course, the opposite is true for the elevated green. A good rule to follow in these two cases is one club less for lower greens, one club more for elevated greens.

As I pointed out before, you're shooting at the green with your other clubs, but with the seven, eight, nine, and wedge you're shooting at the pin. So accuracy is of the utmost importance. There is very little difference in the swing of these four finesse clubs. You use an open stance, you position the ball near the center of the stance with 90 per cent of your weight on the left foot. Make sure both feet stay on the ground throughout the backswing. Turn the shoulders until you're looking at the ball over the left shoulder, keeping the head still and the eyes on the ball. *Don't* use the hip turn. Keep the right elbow close to the body during the backswing. The wrists should cock when the hands reach an area about hip high. Swing in a more upright position, but swing from inside the line of flight. On the downswing move the left shoulder away from the chin, and at this point the left leg should be starting to brace. On the normal shot hit downward sharply on the ball to get it in the air as quickly as possible; this, in turn, will give it more backspin. And after impact point follow through relatively full, but not as high as on distance shots.

As we've stated before, there should be little body motion with the short irons. The closer you get to the hole the more you should concentrate on stillness. Excess body motion will cause the shot to flutter and veer as a result of the different positions of the clubface at impact. A little fade doesn't hurt with the short irons.

The ball line is important. I walk up from behind the ball and place the clubhead down along the desired flight line. When you have done this, adjust your feet in relation to the ball and the clubhead, locking yourself into the correct position.

In conclusion: While the short irons are easier to manipulate for the amateur, no golfer can afford to depend too heavily on one family of clubs. And while the amateur figures he can handle these clubs fairly well, only practice and more practice will prove that the long irons are just an extension of these shorter clubs.

11 THE MIDIRONS (FOUR, FIVE, AND SIX)

As I pointed out in the previous chapter, the lofted clubs (seven, eight, nine, and wedge) are for accuracy. With these irons you're shooting for the pin. In this chapter we're going into the midirons (four, five, and six), used when you're shooting for an area, the middle of the green mostly.

Now, one of the most important aspects of the midirons is alignment. Here you have to pick out an area, an obstacle, a tree, or a bunker with which to line up your shot. You're more than 100 yards away, and the pin can project some faulty clues as to where your shot should land.

As you go up the line with the longer clubs, you'll find that they are tougher to handle; in other words, you can't control them as you do the shorter irons. Of course, I'm speaking about the 15-handicapper. Through practice and more practice, the pros have learned to use these clubs just as any other. And again I want to impress on you that the longer irons are just an extension of the shorter ones. If you think along these lines, you'll find that the four, five, and six irons can be controlled just as the seven, eight, nine, and wedge can be.

Let's take the five iron first. The average golfer will hit this club when he's about 150 yards from the pin. And since there's about ten yards' difference in each club, you'll use the six iron when you're 140 yards away, and the four iron when you're about 160 yards out.

The vital key to these irons is the first 12 to 20 inches in the take-away. Because of the longer shaft you have more margin for error—in other words, the clubface can easily open or close, causing a hook or slice. Take the club back as you would a putter, slowly and close to the ground, making sure the clubface doesn't open or close in this initial effort. This will assure more control at the top of the backswing and down through the impact area.

Now, don't try to get control by taking a shorter grip on the club. If you do this, it will shorten your arc and, naturally, cut down on your distance. In hitting these irons make sure your toes don't move away from your original alignment from point of address to finish. Maintaining the same position is vital to proper balance, so *don't* move your head.

Unlike the long irons (two and three), the middle irons are

WITH THE MIDIRONS THE
TAKE-AWAY AND BACKSWING
ARE VITAL. . . . MAKE IT LOW
AND SLOW. . . . AND SINCE
YOU'RE NOW GOING FOR
DISTANCE, YOUR LEGS
COME INTO PLAY.

neither too stiff nor too whippy. Their length encourages a comfortable address position. You're not going to stand too far from the ball, nor are you going to bend excessively at the knees and waist, as you would with the lofted clubs.

Remember, in using the middle irons, to hit the ball with a slight descending stroke. As in all your shots, the ball should be hit first and the divot should come later. The descending stroke comes naturally if simple fundamentals are observed. The correct stance with the middle irons has the feet closer to the ball than with the long irons. And your feet are in a slightly open position. You play this shot from the center of your stance. The hands should be ahead of the ball at point of address and throughout the shot.

Don't change the backswing with the four, five, and six irons. The swing should be low and slow, with the arms fully extended until the hands enter the hip area. Now, unlike with the lofted clubs, you *do break your wrists*. Make an effort to keep the knees fairly level when pivoting. The left heel should be lifted only enough to make the action of the pivot comfortable.

Start the downswing in the same manner as the shorter irons but with the hip leading the turn to the left. *Don't* lock the left leg. The wrists should remain cocked until they are slightly below the hips. The follow-through should be full, with the arms extended.

THE MIDIRONS (FOUR, FIVE, AND SIX) **51**

We talked about alignment earlier. This is important since most iron shots are doomed to fly off line from the beginning because the weekend golfer is careless about lining up the clubface. As in all my shots, I walk up behind the ball and lay the clubface down in direct line toward the target right behind the ball. Then I plant my right foot at right angles to the intended flight line of the ball. Next I make sure I grip the club so that the sole (*not* the top edge of the clubhead) is also at right angles to the flight line. Then, regardless of which club I'm using, I put my left foot down to complete a square stance, where the line across the toes of my shoes will parallel a line from the ball to the target. Once the stance is completed and you're ready for the take-away, it's important that you check the line once or twice. Pay particular attention to the clubface, *not* the top edge of the club. Then just use the basics to complete the shot.

Many golf courses include terrain that features a number of elevated greens. As you know, this requires a high, feathery shot. One simple adjustment provides the needed height. With a five iron, I play the ball nearly off my left heel instead of just ahead of center. This forward positioning enables the clubhead to meet the ball a little later in the swing, thus increasing the club's effective loft at impact.

Now, say the green is below your ball level. You change from

SIDEHILL WITH BALL ABOVE FEET
YOUR WEIGHT IS SLIGHTLY FORWARD. . . . YOU CHOKE UP ON THE CLUB. . . . REACH OUT FOR THE BALL. . . . USE A THREE-QUARTER SWING FROM THE INSIDE OUT, AND FROM 150 YARDS AWAY AIM ABOUT 20 YARDS TO THE RIGHT TO ALLOW FOR THE DRAW.

SIDEHILL WITH BALL BELOW FEET

STAND CLOSER THAN NORMAL WITH YOUR HEAD
ALMOST DIRECTLY OVER THE BALL. BEND FROM THE WAIST
AND KEEP THE ARMS AND HANDS CLOSE TO THE BODY.

KEEP THE WEIGHT ON THE HEELS AND USE A
THREE-QUARTER SWING. THE SWING SHOULD BE UPRIGHT.
THE BALL WILL FADE RIGHT SO LINE UP LEFT OF TARGET.

53

UPHILL LIE
FLEX THE LEFT KNEE SO YOU ARE IN BALANCE. PLAY THE BALL IN THE
MIDDLE OF YOUR STANCE WITH THE HANDS SLIGHTLY AHEAD. AGAIN,
USE ONLY A THREE-QUARTER SWING. FAVOR THE LEFT SIDE WITH
YOUR WEIGHT. ALLOW FOR A SLIGHT DRAW AND USE MORE CLUB THAN
USUAL SINCE THE TRAJECTORY OF THE BALL WILL BE HIGHER THAN
USUAL.

DOWNHILL LIE
IN THIS CASE FLEX THE RIGHT KNEE. PLAY THE BALL BACK
ON THE RIGHT FOOT. USE LESS CLUB SINCE YOUR
TRAJECTORY WILL BE LOWER THAN USUAL. ALLOW FOR A
SLIGHT FADE AND USE A THREE-QUARTER SWING.

a five to a six iron and hit a "runner." For the runner, I close my stance a little—*not* drastically—by pulling back my right foot. Since the ball will draw from right to left, I aim it to right of the center of the fairway, or a slight bit to the right of the pin. I keep the same grip but use a full swing, with a long, low take-away and backswing.

Because my stance is closed, I will take more of an inside-out-side swing. As I come through the ball, I let my right hand turn over slightly to impart more draw on the shot. At the same time, it is necessary that the right shoulder swings well down under the chin on the downswing. I also use this shot whenever there's any special trouble on the left side of the fairway.

One of the real bugaboos for the 15-handicapper is the uneven fairway lie. You know, any of those uphill, downhill, sidehill lies that make the player feel tilted and out of balance. With a few basic steps, I'll show you how easy it is to make these "impossible" shots just as if you were standing on a level fairway.

The most important thing about these out-of-balance shots is to get comfortable so you feel as though you were hitting from an even surface. To achieve this level feeling, the player should do the following: On a downhill lie the right leg is flexed to level you, and on an uphill lie the left leg is flexed to level you. Next, the player should follow the contour of the ground when he swings. If the golfer feels level himself and then swings as though he really were level, he runs a good chance of missing the shot completely. But if he feels level and swings along the contour of the ground, he's bound to come up with solid contact every time.

A few for-instances: On a sidehill lie with the ball above the feet, you address the ball with your weight a little forward of center. Reach out to the ball and choke up on the club. Swing back inside, following the contour of the ground. Use a three-quarter swing with the left hand pulling toward your target in the follow-through. At 150 yards you should aim about 20 yards to the right as the ball will hook from this lie.

On a sidehill lie with the ball below your feet, stand closer than usual so that your head is directly over the ball. Bend from the waist and keep your arms and hands pretty close to your body. Keep your weight back on your heels and use about a three-quar-ter swing. The swing will be upright since you're closer to the ball. One of the big problems on this shot is how to keep from dipping down into the ball. All you have to do is keep the swing on the same plane as in the address position. Stay on your heels through-out your swing and let the club do the work. The ball will fade to the right on this shot so you should play it about 10 feet to the left of your target.

On the uphill lie, flex the left knee at address until the weight is evenly distributed and you're in balance. Play the ball in the middle of your stance with the hands slightly in front. A word of warning: Try *not* to pick the clubhead up too quickly as it will return to the ball at too sharp an angle. Keep the weight favoring the left side. The follow-through should be a sweeping motion up the hill, again following the contour of the ground. Allow for a slight hook and use more club than normal (a four iron from 150 yards) because of the higher trajectory that the ball will get from the uphill lie.

On the downhill lie, the right knee should be flexed so the weight will be evenly distributed. Play the ball back toward your right foot and keep the hands slightly ahead at point of address. Again, as with the uphill lie, follow the contour of the ground on your backswing. A *no-no* is trying to help the ball get into the air on the downswing. Just let the loft of the club take care of this and you'll stay out of trouble. Use less club than usual (a six iron from 150 yards) because of the low trajectory of the ball. Allow for a slight fade when lining up on your target.

A good point for review while discussing the midirons is the right shoulder action. As you know, there's a natural tendency for the right shoulder to be too high coming through the ball and over the top of the ball on the downswing. One reason for this is that the average right-handed person has an inherent left-side weakness and may put the right side into the swing too soon. As a result, the wrists uncock too soon (at the top of the backswing), and this throws the right elbow out too far, causing an outside-in swing.

Probably the best way to get across correct shoulder turn is to think of the golf swing as a Ferris wheel. The shoulders preferably should tilt vertically, with the right shoulder passing under the chin at impact and follow-through. Taller players, quite naturally, find it easier to tilt their shoulders more vertically than short golfers. However, short players can make sure that their right shoulder stays low by ascertaining that the club is pulled down by the left arm, with the right elbow securely tucked in close to the body on the downswing.

The correct action on the downswing is a lateral movement of the legs and hips toward the target, starting with the lower body. Starting your swing with the lower body shifts your weight predominantly to your left leg, where it was at its original address position. This action will cause the right shoulder to move down and under the chin instead of out and around it, assuring that your clubface will be on line into the ball and on the proper plane.

Having the correct right shoulder position guarantees a proper follow-through and finish—hands high and club between neck and shoulder. Your right side should be turned into the shot, with the heel and sole of your right shoe perpendicular to the ground.

FROM START TO FINISH

Your head should be tilted to the right. Your eyes never should be level looking at the ball in flight.

As we said in an earlier chapter, the right hand should *never* dominate the swing. But this doesn't mean the player shouldn't use his right hand. A player can hit as hard as he wants with the right hand as long as his *left hand remains in control of the swing,* the left staying ahead of the right on the downswing.

We could go into playing your midirons out of high grass and other trouble shots you might wind up with on the golf course fairways, but we'll save that for a later chapter when we discuss all the trouble shots.

A couple of parting reminders about the midirons—four, five, and six. Remember, you're playing for the green, not the pin. Be sure to align the shot with the heel of the club, *not* the top edge. The key to hitting these three clubs is the first 12 to 20 inches in the take-away. We discussed "leveling" the course, so you'll know how to handle downhill lies, uphill lies, and sidehill lies. When playing for elevated greens, play the ball off the left heel so the clubface meets the ball a little later in the swing. The opposite is true when you're hitting a low shot. When you're using the middle irons, be sure to hit the ball with a descending stroke. Remember, the ball first and then the divot. You *do* break your wrists. *Don't* lock the left leg. Your wrists should remain cocked until about hip level on the downswing. The follow-through should be full, with the arms extended. And, finally, control of the right shoulder movement is a must.

THE MIDIRONS (FOUR, FIVE, AND SIX)   **57**

In the next chapter we'll finish out the irons with the big ones —the two and three. Oh, yes, there's the driving iron, and we'll discuss that too. In the meantime don't forget to practice. That's the key to the entire series.

The Long Irons
(One, Two, and Three)

We're getting into the power clubs now. With the one, two, and three irons you let it all hang out—get everything into it that you can. This, of course, holds true through the woods, which we'll take up in the following chapter.

We're not going to spend too much time with the one, or driving, iron, since it's not used as much today as it was a few years ago. Sam Snead was a master with this iron. Sure, you'll see it hauled out on occasion, and by none other than Jack Nicklaus, but on the whole the one iron has just about seen its day.

Why use the one iron in the first place? Mostly for accuracy on a long, tight hole is the logical answer. And the one iron is used off the tee more than not. Say you have a 400-yard par-four hole that is bounded by water on the left and trees on the right. Throw in a couple of fairway bunkers, and this is where the one iron comes out of the bag.

You hit the one iron just as you'd hit the driver. Full backswing, extended arms, the whole power shot. I have used the one iron on occasion. And I hit it just as I hit the woods—fully coiled body on the backswing with a gradual unwinding as I start into the downswing. I leave my wrists cocked up to the final split second before I hit the ball. Concentrating on this delayed uncocking gives me the generating power for my long game.

Another weapon I use with the long clubs are my knees. While I use a lot of body, it's the knees that give me that extra spring off the tee. Most high handicappers are afraid to use the lower part of their bodies (from the hips down) after completing the backswing. By not using these muscles (by swinging stiff-kneed) such players rob themselves of much power.

My swing fundamentals are fairly simple. On the backswing the body should turn freely and far enough so that the hands move over the right shoulder. On the downswing there should be the feeling of the upper part of the body staying behind the ball. At the same time the left hip moves a little toward the target and then twists out of the way. Thinking of the delayed hit (impacting the ball at the moment the wrists are fully released) is a great help.

Halfway through the swing both arms are fully extended. My right shoulder has moved well under my chin and my left leg is strongly braced, absorbing the force of the swing. I make it a point to keep my left side anchored. As the clubhead whips through the shot, the shoulders turn past the 90-degree mark with the hips facing the target at completion of the swing.

As with the woods, I play the long irons fairly forward. In other words, off my left heel. As in my shorter irons, I place the heel of the club behind the ball in direct line with the target. I then step around, go into the waggle, and get comfortable before going into the shot.

One of the main points in power golf is the right elbow. You've got to have it close to the body when you're coming through the downswing. If the right elbow moves in close, the swing has to be an inside-outside effort. If the right elbow flies out and away from the body, the clubhead has to go from outside-in, thus producing a slice. With the right elbow close, you can swing through the shot with both hands with full power and free movement.

We explained earlier that you try to put everything into these long irons. Let's back up a moment. I don't mean swinging with all your might. As I've explained, golf isn't the strong man's game. It's a game of finesse even with the long clubs. Rhythm and tempo are musts. Don't let foolish pride harm your game. If you think the shot calls for a two or three iron, take the two. Most amateur golfers will end up short of their target because they wanted to show their playing partners they could do it with a more lofted club. Playing the less elevated club gives you a more relaxed feeling. You really don't have to use it all to make the club do the work.

Another point I'd like to make here is "staying in motion" at the point of address. Too many 15-handicappers will stand too long over the ball without moving. When you go into your waggle, keep moving from side to side as you size up the target. This causes the muscles in the arms and legs to stay loose. Then, when the backswing starts, you'll be able to make the big turn without tension restricting you.

Let's go back to aligning. When I find I'm getting a little off center with my shots, I go to the practice tee and straighten it out by using the "club alignment system." Place one club on a line with your target and another perpendicular to the first. Then place your toes parallel to the first club. The position of the second club varies with the club you're hitting. In this case if you were using the three iron, you'd line up with the left heel. Then pick out a spot a few yards toward and directly in line with your target. Line up the clubface with it. This procedure may feel strange at first, but, believe me, it works.

The follow-through will always show the results of perfect alignment. The shoulders will rotate under the chin correctly, and the clubhead will return to the square position. There will be

AT THE TOP

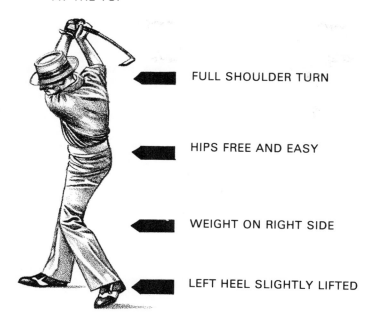

FULL SHOULDER TURN

HIPS FREE AND EASY

WEIGHT ON RIGHT SIDE

LEFT HEEL SLIGHTLY LIFTED

COMING DOWN

SHOULDERS COMING AROUND

LEFT SIDE CLEARING AND SOLID

WEIGHT SHIFTING TO LEFT SIDE

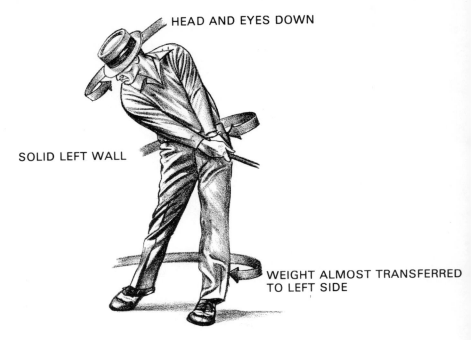

HEAD AND EYES DOWN

SOLID LEFT WALL

WEIGHT ALMOST TRANSFERRED TO LEFT SIDE

no panic signal for last-second correction as in the case when the clubhead is open at point of address. At the finish of your swing your weight should be evenly distributed and your hands will be in a high position.

Most high-handicappers get confused as to the best way to start the backswing with these long irons. They read about restricting the hips on the backswing, but when they try it, it leads to too much hands and arms. There is practically no use made of the legs. The best way for the 15-handicapper to start his swing is simply to think of moving his left knee sideways to the right, with the left shoulder, arms, and club following its lead. You'll find this method a key to a smooth swing.

Now let's take the full swing from start to finish with a two iron. The foundation is footwork and balance. At address, your weight definitely should not be forward on the balls of your feet. It should be shaded toward the heels and evenly distributed in the inside of each foot.

On the backswing about 80 per cent of your weight shifts to the right foot, which is firmly planted. The left foot rolls over to the inside. The left heel may leave the ground just slightly. Amateurs make the mistake of raising the left heel several inches. This pulls the head and body away from the shot and leads to some weird happenings.

On the downswing the weight flows smoothly and unhurriedly to the left side and the left foot resumes its original position. The right foot now rolls over to the inside, and the heel might start leaving the ground at point of impact. Good balance throughout the swing stems from proper footwork, rhythm, and timing.

Before going into the take-away, there are a couple of little motions you should perform. The first is the waggle, which is waving the clubhead over the ball two or three times. Then you set the clubhead down in back of the ball and make the second movement—the forward press. This triggers the swing. You move the right knee in toward the left about an inch. Then you return the knee to its original position, the hands and club go with it, and you go into your backswing.

The backswing is a turn, *not* a sway. Your head and body should remain almost over the ball. The swing is a tilt and a turn, not a sway and a lunge, which most once-a-weekers make out of it. The hips and shoulders turn smoothly and slowly, and your eyes are glued to the ball. The left shoulder tilts and eventually tucks itself under the chin at the top of the backswing.

In the perfect golf swing there should be just the slightest pause at the top. This is where the club changes directions, and too-fast an action could cause the wrists to uncock. The position at the top of the backswing is important. If you have done everything right up to this point, you will be poised and set to go into your smooth downswing. The hands should be high, the body coiled but not swaying to the right. The head is directly over the ball. The weight is on the inside of the right foot, and the left heel is about an inch off the ground, if at all. If you have the proper grip at this point, you will find that the club is resting on the left thumb, directly under the shaft. The club should be almost horizontal.

The secret to long hitting—and this is what you're looking for with the long irons—is to accelerate the clubhead speed on the downswing gradually and delay the uncocking of the wrists until the hands pass the hipline. The first movement at the top of your backswing is the turning of the hips. This brings around the shoulders, arms, and hands in one easy motion.

Early in the downswing the right elbow should return to the right side. This helps delay the uncocking of the wrists. This also allows the inside-outside swing. As we said before, a floppy elbow will get you into trouble every time. At this point the thinking golfer will be able to feel that his left hand and arm are in control until impact. Tucking the right elbow in close to the side certainly promotes this feeling.

As the hands enter the hitting area, the wrists uncock and the clubhead lashes the ball. The uncocking of the wrists must be a natural action. The golfer who starts down correctly won't have

THE LONG IRONS (ONE, TWO, AND THREE) **63**

to worry about his hands and wrists; they'll do their work automatically.

In order for the clubhead to have the proper inside-outside path at impact, the shoulders must tilt and turn at a sufficient angle. If the shoulder turn is too level, the golfer will swing over the ball, never getting that good "thwack" sound that comes with the solid hit. At impact the right shoulder should pass directly under the chin as the clubhead goes through the ball.

Once most of the weight has been transferred to the the left side on the downswing, a player must *not* allow his body to sway toward the target. Those golfers with the proper swing set up a firm left side and then merely swing past it. With this braced "left wall," the left leg is not necessarily straight. The knee does bend slightly toward the target, but it is by no means loose and rubbery.

While your left hand must remain firm and in control at impact, it's at this point that you bring your right hand into the action. Hang on with the left hand and use your right hand forcefully is what I say. Don't make the mistake of overdoing this hand action, or you may destroy your timing.

Drive the back of your left hand toward the target for as long as you can after impact; this keeps the clubhead on a low, controlled arc. It's good to give a slight push-off with the right foot, keeping the left side firm. This will also give you additional power. If the swing has been properly executed, you will be able to hold your balance at the finish for three or four seconds. If you can't do this, you'd better start over again.

I seldom use more than 90 per cent of my power in the long irons. Of course, I'm not advising a lazy swing, but you can control the swing much more easily if you haven't thrown everything into it.

That ends the irons, except for the putter, of course. So the next chapter will be tunneled toward the big bombers, the woods. Don't forget, keep practicing!

13 THE WOODS

Most people think of the woods as the real power clubs in the bag. And they are, if you're thinking about the driver and the two and three woods. But did you know you can get an entire sackful of woods, from the driver to the wedge? That's right! I've even seen a wooden putter.

I realize that I haven't got what you'd call a "picture swing." But I *do* have a solid stroking position at point of impact. I get everything I have into the swing—left side, right side, all of it. Of course, the most important part of the power swing is the *solid left wall.*

This isn't very difficult to learn. Any golfer, large or small, male or female, can utilize this solid left wall to improve his or her game. Let me caution you, however, against too much change, especially if the change isn't natural. There are many different steps in building this left wall. And there are many steps involved in correct execution. Only practice will help you develop this.

The important factor is not to break that solid left side under any consideration. Most professionals agree that the solid left side is a must for a successful golf swing. A golfer may have many faults, but if his left side is solid, he'll always have a pretty fair swing. The braced left side is what I call the payoff. Your grip, your stance, your take-away and backswing and downswing may be perfect, but if your left side collapses, you're in trouble.

The straight left wall begins at the top of the left shoulder and continues down to the left foot. When I say straight, I mean it literally. The worry is not about the head or the hands, but about the body. It should be perfectly vertical.

As you are practicing, you'll begin to notice that you're starting to dig your right foot into the surface of the turf. You dig in with the inside sole of the shoe. This is very important, because digging in your right foot gives you the thrust and power you need for distance hitting.

The positioning of the left foot also is important. At the conclusion of the swing, especially with a smaller player, the left foot should be in the same position as at the start of the swing. And that left foot must be planted. If you move the left foot just a little, the wall moves out of position and you end up with a bad shot.

I cannot stress this point too much—for smaller golfers, that is.

During the downswing the left foot serves as a brace. If the brace breaks, so does the swing. For the normal-size golfer, I recommend that the left foot remain almost straight.

We've discussed the grip in a previous chapter. I use the Vardon (overlapping), but if the baseball grip or the interlocking grip is more comfortable, use it. Too many beginners read too many books and try to do exactly what the book says. That is a mistake. Books should be used only as a general guide. The best grip for you is the one that feels the most comfortable.

There also are three main stances—the square, the closed, and the open. In the square stance you place your feet exactly along the intended flight of the ball. Point the toes slightly out and distribute your weight evenly. In the closed stance you drop the right foot slightly back from the intended flight line. This causes the hips and body to swing slightly to the right. In the open stance your left foot is drawn slightly back, causing the hips and body to face slightly to the left.

I use the open stance with my left foot back from the imaginary line of flight. My right foot is about an inch outside my right shoulder. This is especially good for smaller players who use a lot of leg action. For the average man I suggest a stance no wider than the shoulders. Anything wider might restrict a full shoulder and hip turn.

Many pros have commented on the position of my right knee and my head and eyes at point of address. The right knee is actually bent toward the left leg. I always keep my head about 6 inches in back of the ball and tilted slightly to the right. I concentrate on looking at the ball with my left eye, and I keep this eye on the ball throughout my entire backswing and downswing.

Let me straighten out one misconception at this point. It is a fallacy that the head must remain absolutely still on each shot. This is physically impossible if you want to get anything into a wood shot. Now, I'm not saying you should swing and sway à la Sammy Kaye. You try to keep the head as still as possible, but you'll find you have to move into the ball with the power clubs, and when you do, that head is bound to follow.

At address my left arm is extended and relatively relaxed. My right arm is completely relaxed and tucked into my side. My right shoulder is lower than my left. On the backswing I use a slow turn. I don't particularly concentrate on taking the club back with my hands. I just think of a good 45-degree-angle turn of the shoulders and the hips. My body during the backswing is moving laterally off the ball to the right. This increases the distance the clubhead travels on the backswing and gives me the arc of a much bigger man.

At this point I'd like to clear up another misconception—the straight left arm. You've heard it time and again from one duffer to another: "You're not keeping your left arm straight!" Sure, you try to keep the left arm as rigid as possible, and it *has to be rigid* at point of impact. But when you're going through your waggle at the beginning of the swing, you don't have to be all tied up in making sure the left arm is straight. Again, relaxation is the key —whatever feels more comfortable. But make sure the left arm is part of the solid left side when you actually swing through the shot.

When you take the club back, take it back very low to the ground. Your knees are bent ever so slightly, and when the club reaches the top of your backswing, you're in a semicrouch. At this point, in my case, my left knee has moved well to the right of the ball and I eventually come off my left heel—much more so than an average-size man. This additional leg turn is essential to my swing in that it allows me to coil the muscles in my right thigh and reach the fullest extension possible of my left arm and the muscles of the upper back. This then, is how I generate the power in my downswing. Again, let me say that this is for the smaller man. The big guy doesn't have to go into this exaggerated leg movement.

When I'm at the top of my backswing, I pause slightly. This is to allow my muscles enough time to prime themselves for the full turn into the shot. My left heel is higher off the ground than that of most golfers. I then start my hip turn, and about halfway into the downswing I throw my right shoulder into the swing. Now my left heel is planted solidly, and my wrists are still cocked. My left arm is straight; so is my left leg. From this point on, the solid left wall theory is in play.

At a split second before impact, my wrists uncock and my right arm extends as I go through the ball. My left shoulder moves up rapidly, showing a pronounced tilt and turn of both shoulders. By this time my weight has moved well off the right side. My head position shows that I didn't let it restrict my swing. Although the clubhead has struck the ball only a second earlier, my head now begins to come up.

Extremely important now is that my left leg is still braced so it can absorb the force of the swing. The wall is strong. Again a word of caution—this is my way of hitting the power shot. I elaborated on my game in the first part of this chapter to show that, although I go through the exaggerated leg and hip movements, basically I'm the same at point of impact as any average-size man.

Something else I'd like to mention at this time. If you've ever seen me play in a tournament, you will have noticed that I tee the ball very high and never drag the clubhead along the ground on my take-away. My theory on this is that many times you have a

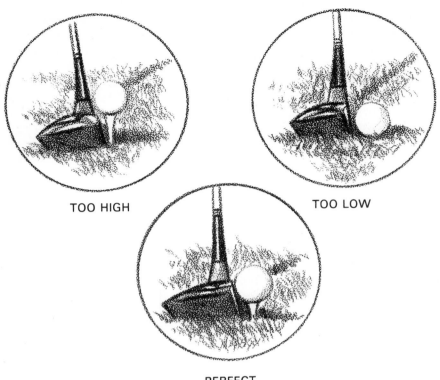

TOO HIGH

TOO LOW

PERFECT

tendency to lift the club after heeling it. So by teeing the ball high I can bring the clubhead back with that low, rhythmic feeling.

Good arm extension is vital to good golf. The good golfer finishes with his hands high and the clubhead well over his left shoulder. His right side will be fully turned toward the target with his belt buckle facing the target. And he'll be up on his right toe. Getting the arms and hands into the downswing too soon can result in poor extension and loss of power. There is a tendency among 15-handicappers to try to increase clubhead speed by using the hands too soon. A strong hitter will hold the relationship between the left arm and the club shaft that was established at the top of the backswing.

A good player starts his downswing with his lower body—hips and then legs. Then the arms, hands, and clubhead follow for proper timing. The left hand remains in control of the club as the left side pulls the right side through the shot. The left hand stays in front of the right hand until after impact. The left hip slides toward the target and turns clear just before impact.

If you'll observe all the touring pros, you'll see that they all get the club as far from their body as possible just after impact. There is a full extension of the right arm, and the left arm is almost fully extended. Most high-handicappers will not fully extend their right arm coming through the ball. There is definitely a loss of power and consequently a loss of distance.

Weaker hitters are characterized by the collapse of the arms—their elbows are separated, with the left elbow bowed out. The bowed left arm results in lost leverage, and that means loss of distance and causes shanking. Another fault of the weaker hitters is quitting at impact point. They seem to think that after hitting the ball there's no point in following through. All good golfers hit through the ball. Full extension of the arms at the impact point is important in accomplishing this aspect of the swing.

While the left elbow should *not* be bowed out at impact point, this doesn't mean that the left wrist *shouldn't* be bowed out. The left wrist should be bowed out and facing the target rather than breaking in. So if you concentrate on a full extension of both arms at impact, you'll add at least 25 yards to your drives.

You know, I keep hounding one and all about the necessity of practicing. But I haven't gone into the subject very deeply. Such as when to practice. The best time by far is *after* a round of golf. Then your body is warmed up and your muscles relaxed. A good warming-up exercise consists simply of swinging the club back and forth, slowly at first and then more rapidly as you go along. Do this for about five minutes and you'll find your muscles are ready to go the full route of all your clubs in the bag.

Actually the fairway woods are more important than your driver. While you can get up there on the tee and whale away indiscriminately, you need a greater degree of accuracy in hitting from the fairway. In other words, with the driver all you have to think about is keeping the ball in play. With the fairway woods you stamp an image of the perfect shot in your mind even as you select your club. You have to consider such things as trouble on the left or right, bunkers, water, whether the green is soft or hard, which way the wind is blowing, whether the green is tilted away from you or toward you, whether the pin is on the right, left, at the front or at the back of the green.

In thinking through the fairway wood shot, the key question to ask yourself is: "Can I make the green?" If you decide you can't reach it, the next question should be: "Where do I want this shot to end up so I'll have an easy pitch to the pin?" It's usually on a par-five hole that you need a wood for your second shot, and if you can get your pitch near the hole, you have a chance for a birdie.

There is a tendency for the 15-handicapper to play all fairway wood shots the same way—usually off the left instep or left toe. Actually this is good thinking when the ball is sitting up. But if you're in a divot or on a sidehill lie, you have to do some shifting

THE COMPLETE PICTURE

around. We discussed this in the chapter on the long irons, and it's a good policy to use the same format with the woods.

But, unlike the long irons, your fairway wood shots at the point of impact should be hit squarely and *not* on a downward swing. You're not trying to put bite on the ball—you're trying to hit the ball as far as possible with as much roll as possible. Now, if you have a chance of reaching the green with the wood, you should put a slight fade on your shot; the ball hitting the green will hold better. To put this fade on the shot, you open your clubface at address. Your left foot is drawn back about an inch from the line of flight. Make sure your left hand is in control when you take the club back slightly outside the normal line of your swing. Then bring the clubface down and across the ball.

If you want a run, or hook, on the ball, naturally you're going to have to line up differently. For the draw, or hook, you draw your right foot back from the flight line about an inch. Then you'll swing through as you ordinarily do, and the inside-outside swing will maneuver the ball just the way you want it to go.

Now, the high-handicapper usually hits a fairway wood better than his two or three iron, so naturally, he'll haul out the wood when he has to make a decision as to whether to use the wood or the iron. Some touring pros have dropped the two iron and added a five wood. It gives about the same distance and provides you with an added advantage of having another, easier club to hit in your arsenal. Again, it's just a matter of getting used to any club, and that can be accomplished only by practice.

Much has been said about whether to hit an iron or a wood out of the rough. This, of course, is according to where your ball is sitting. If it's down under, so to speak, the iron is your best bet. But, on the average lie, I'd rather take a wood any time. Just to see what club is easier to draw through grass, take out a two iron and a four wood and swing it through the grass. You'll be surprised to find that the wood swings much more easily than the iron.

I said earlier that I use about 85 per cent of my swinging power on most shots. The seemingly fast swing of the average pro comes from the "cranking up" process that begins with the forward press and continues through the downswing and ends at the top of the swing in what seems to be a split second of fury. But it's not really all that involved. The average pro, including myself, very seldom puts everything into a shot.

Let me tell you, power comes from practice. Basic fundamentals, refined into a grooved swing that you can depend on when you address any situation, must be mastered prior to turning it on. Until you are satisfied that you have all the elements of the swing under control, you will be much happier if you swing easy, stay loose and comfortable, and let your clubs do the work. Only when you are completely in control of your game can you expect to realize your potential.

Another thing that really boggles the imagination is winter rules. Winter rules allow the high-handicapper at public courses to move his ball around on the fairway—and in the rough, for that matter—to where the ball is sitting up as if it were on a tee. This is a bad deal. When the ball is sitting up, you lose one of the basic concepts of golf—keeping the head down and swinging through the ball. If you play the ball as it lies, you will discover a challenge toward improvement. This will ultimately reduce your handicap, and eventually you will attack each shot with confidence.

Naturally, there are times when impossible lies must be corrected. However, if you had the opportunity to call for a ruling each time you got in this situation, you would find very few officials who would concur. Confidence gained by executing one of these "impossible" shots caused by a bad lie is of great value. Great concentration is demanded by this situation. And concentration is one of the most important keys in the game of golf.

In the first place, you must make contact with the ball first, regardless of where it's lying. The shot from a less-than-desirable lie requires the full clubface value as opposed to the common way of hooding or repositioning of the hands. A slightly exaggerated crouch (knee bend) will help you stay down on this shot. This is important to avoid sculling or topping the shot.

Dry grass conditions with hard pan underneath should be approached from a square stance. Face left of the target to compensate for a possible slice. Good balance is important. Generally the ball is to be positioned in the middle of the feet. Avoid having the hands too far ahead of the ball. The swing should be upright. A strong left-side pull will bring the clubhead into the ball sharply, which is essential. The follow-through is high and extended, as in any ordinary shot. We'll go into this type of shot more thoroughly in the chapter on trouble shots.

That's practically the whole bag—the finesse clubs, the mid-irons, the long irons, and the woods. Our next chapter will be on the one aspect of the game that everyone handles differently. It surely is the part of the game that can take off many strokes. It's putting—the bugaboo of the touring professionals.

14 PUTTING

Somebody said that putting was 90 per cent in the head. I'll agree up to a point. I know that when I'm putting well, I'm playing well. But that's only natural. You're certainly not going to score if you're missing those three- and four-footers.

I know there are as many different theories on putting as there are golfers. But a few basics are neccessary if you want to control the putter. Reading the green is one basic. Is it fast, slow, or medium? Then there are the breaks in the green, the problem of keeping the head and body as still as possible, of not watching the ball drop into the cup.

Let's start from the beginning. Thinking positively is a big part of putting. If you think that hole is as big as a watermelon, then you're going to make a lot of "snakes." If you go up to your ball and have a bad attitude, you're certainly not going to make the long ones, or the shorter ones, either.

One of the main factors in my putting is keeping the weight on my left foot. This insures my balance. I also keep my eyes on the back of the ball throughout my putting stroke. I try to keep my body and head absolutely motionless. As in my other shots, I believe in putting fast. The guy who hesitates over his ball for long periods is bound to get nervous. And a nervous putter just doesn't sink any putts.

On all putts I read the break and the rub of the green from all angles. Then just before I step up to the ball to putt, I kneel behind the ball and cup my hands behind my eyes. This is to block out everything around me except the ball and the cup. In fact, it's like putting blinders on a race horse. Then I step up to the ball and putt it with a smooth and rhythmic stroke. I never see the ball go into the cup. That's right—I hear it! I know this is difficult, but if you practice this way you'll learn to keep your head down and your body motionless throughout the stroke.

Your grip on the putter should be the result of much trial and error on the practice green. This is especially so when you're first beginning to play golf. Once you've found the right grip, the one that suits you best, never change. The worst thing a golfer can do is to keep experimenting with his grip on the putter. The best thing is to adopt a grip that's most comfortable, then practice it

until it becomes completely second nature. This, of course, includes the stance and stroke.

I use a more pigeon-toed stance than most. This is to steady my body. Most good putters won't lift the club more than half an inch off the green on the backswing. And, speaking of backswings, keep it as short as possible. Of course, this depends on distance, but as in bowling, less movement makes for fewer errors. Putters with exaggerated backstrokes greatly increase their chances for error.

Reading the green is as important to your game as the stroke itself. You should become familiar with the green as soon as you step on it for the first time. You can tell if it's hard or soft just by walking on it. Then check the texture of the grass to see if it's fine or coarse. Another thing about checking the texture, you must do this on every hole. Textures change not only from course to course, but from hole to hole.

If it's not your turn to putt, use this time to study the other player's shot. From it you can tell how the ball is going to roll and in what direction. You must also determine whether or not the green is grainy. When you're putting against the grain, naturally you must hit the ball harder. Grainy greens are those in which the grass lies flat, not upright. When the sun is out, you can detect a shine in the direction the grain runs. On courses near water, the grain usually runs toward the water.

After reading the green, you must determine the line of flight you want your ball to take. Another little tip: First thoughts are best. If you're having trouble confirming the line, go to the back of the hole and survey the situation from that angle. If the putt is extremely long, go to a point equidistant from ball and hole. You should be able to find any slope from this spot.

Once you've determined the line, concentrate on that one point and nothing else. Get up to the ball, stroke it confidently, and you should have few problems. It's the second-guessers, the ones who make the scenes on the green, who usually wind up in trouble.

A good putting stroke has a definite arc. The ball should be stroked just at the bottom or slightly on the upswing of that arc. An ideal putting stroke is like a pendulum going back and forth. The toe and heel of the club should swing through at the same time. Most missed putts are the result of the heel leading the toe or the toe leading the heel at point of impact.

In making contact with the ball, it's important that the hands lead the putter through the stroke and that the wrists don't break. Of course, the type of stroke is up to the individual golfer. It doesn't matter if you use a stiff-wrist shot, which is swung more with the upper arms and shoulders, or whether you use your wrists predominantly. Whatever feels natural, that's the stance and stroke for you to use.

Distance is a big factor with the good putter. Many high-hand-icappers will roll too far or come up short. Once you master this distance factor—and it takes a lot of practice—your ball will end up close to the hole even if you're off on your direction.

Short putts should be stroked hard enough so that the ball hits in the back of the cup. Many golfers think a short putt should be tapped in rather than stroked. But whatever, the ball on a short putt should be stroked hard enough so that if you miss, you'll be about ten inches past the cup.

The pros have different ideas concerning the length of the backswing. Some deliberately use the short backstroke with a long follow-through after stroking the putt. Whatever way you do it, the backswing should be a swing and *not* a lift, and there should be increasing momentum at point of impact.

The short putt is usually more difficult than the long one. That's because many of you never practice those two- and three-footers. Another fault common in the short putt is lack of acceleration at impact. But when you come right down to thinking about it, it's advantageous to practice the short putts more often than the long ones. It's fairly easy to lag up pretty close to a hole, but once you're there, you still have to sink the putt. Thus, the short putt is always there, while the long ones come and go.

One thing I forgot to mention about greens is weather condi-

COMFORT:
THAT'S THE MAIN THING IN PUTTING

LINING UP

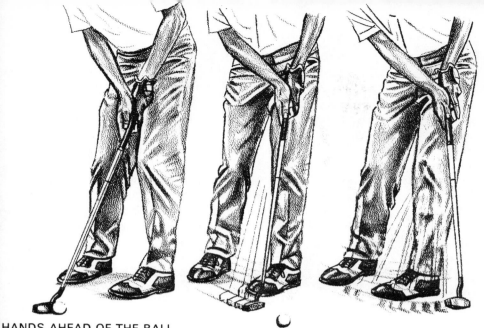

HANDS AHEAD OF THE BALL . . .

. . . WEIGHT ON LEFT FOOT . . .

AND THE STROKE SMOOTH AND RHYTHMIC

M THE FRONT

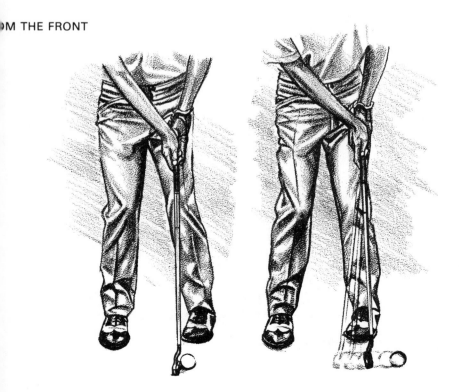

tions. There is less break on wet greens than on dry ones. A firmer stroke is needed, since the ball won't roll as freely. Another factor is that if there is no water around, the grain will run in the direction the wind blows most. This is particularly true in the southwestern part of the United States, and in Florida, where Bermuda grass is prevalent.

One of the most common explanations of bad putting is called the jitters. This is when you can't buy a putt and everything seems to be tumbling down. Naturally, each player must be able to evaluate himself and his ability to solve his problem. Some pros have different versions of how they snapped out of a bad case of the jitters. One fast putter solved his problem by putting slowly. Another, who putted slowly, started putting quickly. It's all up to the individual.

One school of thought has the putter taking practice swings until he's sure of himself and totally relaxed. Another would line up the putt and stroke it. A third would have you manage every putt exactly alike—so many walks around the green each time, so many practice swings, anything you feel like, just so you do the same thing each time. Considering all facets, the third method seems most logical since at least you'll be getting into a groove, which, as you know, is one of the most important phases of the game.

But getting back to the basics, you definitely have to have balance, a solid foundation, and rhythm to be a good putter. There should be absolutely no tension when you're standing over a putt. That way you can tap the ball sharply and smoothly and get good results. And once again let me tell you, for good results you must practice. Nobody can teach anybody how to putt—you're strictly on your own in this department.

As with the rest of your clubs, the putt starts with the grip. I use the reverse overlap grip. I feel that this grip keeps my hands more stable through the stroke. You might say I'm a left-handed putter in that my left hand dominates the stroke, but I try to keep both hands working at all times. The big thing I try to do, especially under pressure, is to keep the putter blade lined up in the right direction. I also keep the blade low, as I said before. I keep a firm grip on the shaft. I play both uphill and downhill putts the same way. It's strictly a matter of tempo.

I like to feel that I swing the putter back with little independent wrist or hand movement. From the top of my backswing, as with my other clubs, I like to get the feeling of a pause before I go into my stroking action. My stroke is primarily an arms and shoulders activity. Sure, there are wrist putters and arm putters, but for me, the best way is the stiff-wrist stroke.

A little tip on your stance. When the wind's blowing, take a slightly wider stance. This enables you to keep a better balance. As you practice, you'll find that after a while you won't think about your stance or your grip or whatever. You'll just become so automated that you'll do all these things without thinking about them. And speaking of practicing, I find the best way is to put a lot of balls in a circle around the hole and work back as far as I want to go.

I know, most players don't like to practice putting. They'd rather go out there on the practice tee and hit the cruncher, the long ball. But you'll find that these aren't the players who are winning the big buck on the tour. More than any other part of your game, putting is the one that takes strokes off your game and puts more money in your pocket.

Getting back to the length of the backswing—this is strictly according to feel. It's like tossing a ball to somebody. If I'm standing close to you, I'm not thinking about how far I'm going to take my hand back to throw to you. It's the same in putting. The farther you're away the longer the backswing. Another part of your stance that is important is standing up. The more upright your stance the better you can look at the hole. Too many players crouch so low that their view of the hole is lowered, and that makes it seem smaller.

When the greens are in perfect shape, you aim at getting as

THE BEST WAY TO PRACTICE . . .
PUT BALLS IN A CIRCLE AROUND THE HOLE.

much roll on the ball as possible. You know the ball is going to roll true, so your stroke should be smooth and rhythmical. But if you have a rough green, you'll want to get the ball into the air, make it bounce. If you want to make it bounce more, you hit down on the ball so it will jump the first eight or ten inches. It's good to use this bounce method late in the day when you find a lot of spike marks on the greens.

You've heard players say they can actually visualize the ball going into the cup when they're having good days. This is a wonderful feeling—knowing the ball is going where you're aiming. But then there are the other days when you just can't get that image, and on those days you're in trouble. "Thinking in" a putt is part of the mental angle of the game.

Another thing I look for in my grip is to have my thumbs run straight up and down the shaft. This allows me to gauge the straightness of my stroke. If your thumbs turn, you know the clubface turned.

Earlier I said I had most of my weight on my left foot. What I'm talking about here is that this gives me a sort of forward press. When you first stand over the ball, you have your hands directly over the ball. Then you allow the hands to move forward about three inches. Take the club back directly from that forward press position. *Do not* bring the hands back to the original position before starting back.

Some of the professionals point their left elbow toward the hole. In other words, the arms are out from the body. Of course, this would turn a lot of weekend golfers into raving maniacs, but it does serve a purpose. With this grip the back of the left hand is pointed directly at the cup. The tendency to turn or flinch is entirely eliminated.

Here are a couple other tips that will help your putting efficiency: Keep your eyes on the back of the ball and line up to the center of the cup, *not* in the general direction. On long putts pick out a blade of grass or a dark patch about 3 feet in front of the ball in direct line with the cup. Then try to putt the ball directly over this spot. Keep a log on how you're missing your putts—left, right, too hard, too soft. You'll find that these tips will let you in on more dollar Nassau bets than you can imagine.

Another thing you might keep in mind: Think of the putting stroke as a pulling action, not a pushing action. The right hand and forearm, along with the putter, are pulled through the ball by the left forearm. The left arm and hand guide the putter to the ball, while the right forearm and hand are allowing the putter head to stroke through the ball. Acceleration (coming through strong at impact point) is the name of the game on all putts. Remember this!

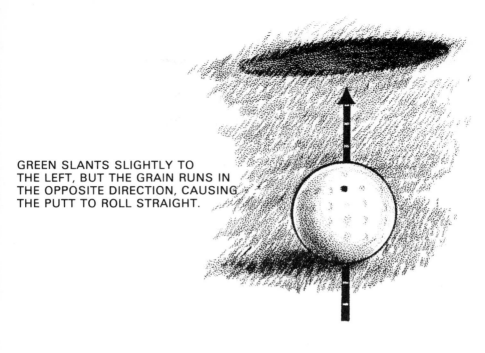

GREEN SLANTS SLIGHTLY TO
THE LEFT, BUT THE GRAIN RUNS IN
THE OPPOSITE DIRECTION, CAUSING
THE PUTT TO ROLL STRAIGHT.

VARIABLES

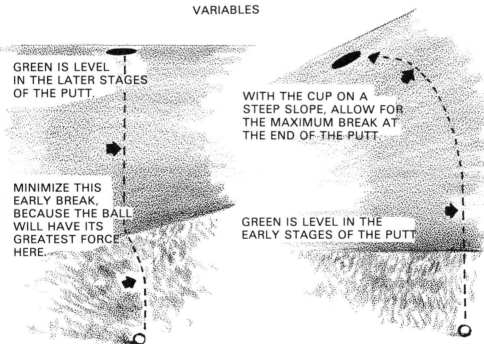

GREEN IS LEVEL
IN THE LATER STAGES
OF THE PUTT.

WITH THE CUP ON A
STEEP SLOPE, ALLOW FOR
THE MAXIMUM BREAK AT
THE END OF THE PUTT.

MINIMIZE THIS
EARLY BREAK,
BECAUSE THE BALL
WILL HAVE ITS
GREATEST FORCE
HERE.

GREEN IS LEVEL IN THE
EARLY STAGES OF THE PUTT

PUTTING WITH GRAIN—USE CAUTION.

PUTTING AGAINST GRAIN—BE BOLD.

Kneeling behind the ball with the putter head square to the ball is the most frequently taught way of reading a green. Some players, however, use the plumb-line method (holding the shaft of the putter with the thumb and forefinger). In the plumb line you let the club hang freely and straight down. You're standing behind the ball and looking toward the cup. Sight with only one eye open, covering the ball with the lower part of the putter shaft.

You should sight with your dominant eye—usually the right for right-handers and the left for left-handers. Of course, you can easily determine your dominant eye by pointing your right index finger at an object about 15 feet away with both eyes open. Close one eye, and if you still seem to be pointing directly at the object, this is your dominant eye. If you close your dominant eye, the object will appear to have moved a few inches to one side.

Still on the plumb-line method: Without moving either your head or your putter, look at the hole. If the hole shows to the right of the shaft, the putt will break to the right by the amount indicated. If it shows to the left, the same thing will happen to the left. Should the top of the shaft block your view of the hole, you have a straight-in shot. The advantage of the plumb-line method is that, worked properly, it can reveal an unseen (through the naked eye) break in the green. In using the plumb-line method, it's a good idea to draw imaginary lines from the hole to the ball.

Another thing I like to feel is that my hands are free. This is why I'm more or less a stand-up putter. This keeps my hands high and makes me feel the putter is an extension of my left arm. This makes it easier for me to keep the blade of the putter square to the ball throughout the stroke.

The high-handicapper has a tendency to keep his eyes on the blade of the putter. This is a fatal practice. You should *never* take your eyes off the back of the ball, which is where you're going to strike it. In addition to *not* moving my head or breaking my wrists, I certainly don't move my legs or knees. I don't believe in bumping short putts—that is, using little or no follow-through. I feel the putting stroke isn't complete if you don't follow through on the shot.

Another point in reading a green. If the green slants slightly to the left but the grain runs in the opposite direction, you have to figure on an almost straight putt. Of course, this depends on the angle of the slope. Also, when the grain runs against you, naturally you have to putt the ball harder. The opposite is true if the grain is with you.

If a first putt overshoots the mark, many players are somewhat timid on return putts. A little nerve will help this situation. For one thing, you'll almost always find the right line on the return putt. Of course, if you were putting with the grain on the first try, remember it will take a little harder putt on the return to the hole.

In most instances you can see the slant of the green well enough to gauge your shot. However, if you are unable to decide on the break, the best solution is to examine the cup itself. If one side of the cup looks lower, then the green does tip toward the low side.

The break depends a lot on the speed of the putt. If the ball is traveling slowly, it will follow whatever break there is in the green. On the other hand, if it's moving fast, its momentum will keep it more in line. The problem of force versus break comes when you're not sure of the amount of break. If you're not sure, a firm putt will sometimes overcome whatever slight break there might be in the green.

Also remember, a ball will break more on a long putt at the end of its roll. So if you're lining up a putt on a slanted green, you'll have to take into consideration the amount of tilt near the ball as compared with the tilt near the hole. If the green is hard, the ball will travel more on top of the grass, causing a full break.

Continuous but smooth movement is the basis of my putting. Once I have decided on the angle and amount of steam I want to put into the stroke, I step up and put my putter down in front of the ball, move it to the back of the ball, and immediately go into the stroke. All of this takes only a few seconds and keeps me tension-free.

One of the big things in putting is *not* quitting on the shot. When I see the putterhead strike the ball and then feel it swing on through still square to the target line, I know I have a good putt. After impact my hands move forward along the target line in a sweeping motion.

Let me insert something here that is very important: your reaction to a missed putt. If you take it too much to heart, you can foul up your entire game. So you blow one . . . forget it! Then go to the next hole with a completely clear mind.

That's it on putting. When you come right down to it, nobody can teach anybody how to putt. All anyone can do is give the basics, which I have attempted to do, and the rest is up to the individual. Lotsa good luck!

The next chapter will deal with sand shots—real bugaboos to the weekend high-handicappers. But when we get through, I'm sure you'll know much more about hitting this shot. I'll let you in one of my little secrets: I'd rather play the ball out of the sand than out of the high grass around the green. I'll tell you why in the next chapter.

15 SAND SHOTS

There are all kinds of sand . . . soft and snowlike, dense, heavy, powdery, just about any kind you (don't) want. I threw that "don't" in there because most weekend golfers would rather face a firing squad than a sand shot. And, really, pitching out of the sand is a relatively easy exercise. But, as in all golf shots, it takes practice.

First, you test the sand. You've seen the pros dig their feet into the sand. Well, that's how you can tell how heavy or light it is. Once you have put it to the test, you plant your feet firmly by digging in. Always use an open stance for trap shots, and, for that matter, any trouble shot. An open stance helps you bring the club-head through against any extra resistance, such as sand, water, or high grass.

When in the sand, use a sand wedge. The wedge has a heavy head and thick bottom. It can cut through sand much more easily than any other club in your bag. On a short shot from dry sand I usually hit about an inch behind the ball. However, if the sand is heavy, as from a heavy rain, I hit much closer than an inch. It's just logical that you *can't* pull the clubhead through the shot as easily if the sand is heavy.

I don't crowd the ball, and I usually play it opposite my left foot. I concentrate on a slow take-away and backswing, and I swing

THERE'S VERY LITTLE BODY ACTION IN A SAND SHOT.
AT POINT OF IMPACT THERE'S THIS FEELING OF
FLICKING AT THE BALL WITH THE HANDS AND WRISTS.
THE HANDS STAY OVER THE BALL ALL THE WAY.

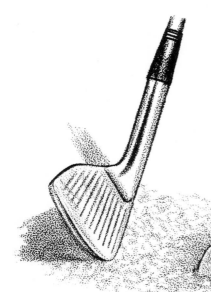

THE PUTTER IS A GOOD CLUB
TO USE OUT OF THE SAND
IF IT'S HARD
AND THERE'S NO LIP.

YOU HIT ABOUT ONE INCH
BEHIND THE BALL.

YOU SWING TO THE LEFT
AS THE SAND WILL
DRAG THE CLUB OPEN
AT IMPACT POINT.

UPHILL LIE . . . LEFT FOOT

DOWNHILL LIE . . . RIGHT FOO

completely through these shots. There can be no babying this shot because you *must* cut through the sand.

When you have a buried lie, close the clubface. *Do not* swing too hard. The ball will come out easily enough without your putting pressure on the swing. Pressure will only distort the swing, with a shank or a pull the probable result.

One of the most—probably *the* most—difficult of all sand shots is the downhill lie. I play this shot off the right foot, and I always allow for a roll because the ball won't have any backspin on it. Again, I hit about an inch behind the ball, and the movement of the club is a sharp, downward blow. You have to cut *under* the ball.

Sure, the sand shot is different from any other in the game. This is because in a sand-shot explosion you don't hit the ball with your club, but with the sand in back of the ball. The force created by the sand wedge causes the ball to pop up and out of the trap and onto the green.

The explosion shot is the easiest way to get out of the sand. Oh, sure, you can use a putter on occasions, but only if there is no lip on the bunker and the ball can be rolled out with no chance of catching on high grass. And you can chip out of a trap. But chipping requires a delicate touch that takes hours and hours of practice to perfect. The pros use the explosion shot almost exclusively on all occasions.

The rules do *not* allow you to ground your club in the sand. The penalty is two strokes in stroke play and loss of hole in match play. At point of address you hold the clubface behind the ball about half an inch above the sand. The ball is played from opposite the left instep to the toes, and the left foot is drawn back from the line of flight. Of course, your feet are firmly planted. Your hips and shoulders are pre-turned to the left in an open stance. This enables you to turn without losing balance on the downswing.

The clubface is laid back to make it easier for the club to cut through the sand and to give the ball a high flight so it will clear whatever lip or obstacle is between you and the cup. Also the high-flight line will enable the ball to settle quickly on the green.

The explosion shot should never be made with a hard swing. This causes loss of balance in the unsettled footing of the sand. Instead the backswing should be no more than a three-quarter exercise. The downswing should be relaxed but firm and rhythmical. And never quit on the shot; the club should keep accelerating. As you practice the explosion shot, you'll find you will be able to adjust to the varying distances. It's up to you and you alone to get the feel of each situation.

As I said in the preceding paragraph, NEVER QUIT ON THE SHOT. The explosion shot requires a full follow-through. There are a couple of ways that you can fail on the sand shot. One is to hit too far behind the ball and bury the clubhead. When you bury the clubhead you naturally quit on the shot, and this kills the follow-through. The other common fault is taking too little sand. This is called "picking it clean" and could result in your ball landing in the next county.

As I've stated before, the closed clubface is the only way to play a buried ball. When you close the clubface, you allow the wedge to cut deeper into the sand than it normally would. Then, swing a little harder, and the force of the downward blow will excavate the ball.

The open stance on an explosion shot is more upright than any other in golf. The position of the right hip, which is turned around toward the target, at point of address prevents the hands from coming back in a flat arc and encourages a quick cocking of the wrists on the backswing. Though the swing is upright, you should avoid raising your body on the backswing. You have to have the feeling of staying down on the shot with the knees flexed and the head anchored.

The nearer you hit behind the ball, the farther the ball will go. In other words, you have to pick the club straight up and hit down. Up and down! You'll be able to gauge these shots much better after some time in the practice bunkers. Another thing I've found is that the good sand players all grip short on the club. The sand-shot swing should be short and definite with the hands and wrists quite firm.

Of course, there are times when you can't use the explosion shot, such as after a heavy rain when the sand gets packed down. This calls for the pitch shot. This shot, like all the finesse shots, takes much practice. You sort of lift the ball out of trouble instead of pushing through on the shot. Now, I'm not talking about scooping the ball. You definitely hit into the ball but with less intensity.

I didn't go into the reason for the open stance on sand shots. The open stance causes the clubhead to move outside its normal arc on the backswing and to slice across the ball at impact. This puts a left-to-right spin on the ball that propels it to the right of the target. It is therefore wise to aim slightly to the left of target when hitting the sand shots. The ball will not spin much, because you hit the sand first and this takes friction away from the ball.

Very little body action is required in the sand shot—just enough to get that feeling of rhythm. And here's another factor in determining the distance of a sand shot—the wider the stance, the shorter the flight of the ball.

At point of impact there should be the feeling that the clubhead never passes the hands. The hands come into the shot and flick the clubhead at the ball. Then the club continues on toward the target, and the hands stay over the ball. The wrists should uncock a little earlier than on fairway shots.

As to lies, there are uphill lies, downhill lies, and sidehill lies. With the uphill lie, the clubhead encounters more sand, and therefore it's necessary to swing harder. The ball should be played well forward (opposite the left foot), similar to the method used on the uphill fairway shot. It's not necessary to try for deep penetration. It is better to lay the clubface open at point of address, which minimizes the amount of sand the clubface will have to encounter.

On the downhill lie, the problem is to get enough sand and let the clubhead cut under the ball. It's easier to do this by closing the clubface so that it will dig deeper into the sand. The ball should be played off the right foot. A word of caution: On this downhill lie with the clubface closed, the ball will fly out of the sand rather low and have little backspin on it. The idea is to get the up-and-down feeling—straight up and straight down.

The big danger in executing the downhill lie (the ball lower than the feet) is raising the body at impact, which causes a topping of the shot. It's therefore necessary to take a longer grip on the club and just play the shot as you would any other out of the sand.

With the ball above the feet, direction comes upon the scene. The tendency is to hit the ball to the left, so you aim to the right to compensate. Here, again, practice will determine how much and how far.

When hitting the ball out of the sand where the lip of the bunker is hanging over the ball, address the ball off your left toe and keep the clubface open wide. Your head must stay behind the ball, and you must follow through on the shot.

If you have a downhill lie at the back of the trap, you play it just the opposite. At point of address you dig your left foot firmly into the sand. Your hands are well ahead of the ball. Take the clubhead back and up sharply to a three-quarter swing with a quick wrist break. *Do not* shift the weight from one foot to the other; keep the weight more on the left side throughout the swing. Use only your hands and arms on this little shot. On the downswing pull the club down into the sand just behind the ball and with *no* follow-through. Also, allow for plenty of roll.

You know, I told you in the preceding chapter that I'd rather play the ball out of the sand than out of the high grass around the green. The reason is that sand almost always has the same degree of consistency, whereas there are many variables in grass. So I'll take my chances on the sand shot with anyone, and I'm sure you will too when you master the shot. And the only way to master any shot is practice.

Actually, terms such as "explosion," "traps," and "bunkers" make the game of golf sound like a war. This scares the average golfer. Sand is just a decoration, a directional guide. Certainly it's nothing to be afraid of. Again, all it takes to master sand shots is practice.

16 TROUBLE SHOTS

Like the sand shot, shots from the high rough and "impossible lies" create consternation among weekend golfers. In this chapter I'm going to show you how to deal with some of these challenges.

A short shot out of high grass is always a pesky thing. You're not too sure how thick the grass is and just how much pressure to put into the shot. So the first thing you have to do is find out how deep and lush the grass is and whether it's entwining or straight. You do this by walking around in the grass near your ball.

You address the ball off your left foot (slightly left of center since you're using a short stance). Now, instead of the low take-away and backswing, you have to lift the club abruptly. You get less resistance and a truer arc on your backswing. Then on the downswing you have less grass to cut through.

I can't emphasize this next point enough: You have to take almost a death grip on the club. If you don't, the grass will literally tear the club out of your hands. Also, you have to be definite in your swing—don't give up on the shot. Open the clubface because the high grass will close it as you come into the ball. For this reason I play the shot slightly to the right. Here again, it takes practice to gauge shots like this, and how many of you ever practice this type of shot?

Most professionals preach using an iron out of deep rough. I disagree! Make this test: Swing an iron in some rough and then swing a lofted wood. You'll find that the wood swings much more easily and you're able to drag the clubhead through the shot with less effort than with the iron. The iron cuts, the wood slides through—it's as simple as that.

In addition to these trouble shots, there's the one when you're under tree branches. In this case, of course, you have to keep the ball low. Address the ball off your right foot and hit the shot with your left hand completely in control. You'll be using a less lofted club, such as a two or three iron or a three wood. You must stay down on this shot more than in any other in golf, with the exception of the sand shot.

And speaking of trees, there's the shot that you can't hit right-handed. In this case you simply use the back of the club and hit it left-handed. It is important to pull the right hand into the ball

in executing this shot. You'll either cut or draw this shot.

Then there's the shot where you have to go over a tree or two. In this circumstance you address the ball off the instep of your left foot. Then you open the clubface and use a more lofted club, preferably a four or five wood for distance, or a nine iron or wedge for a shorter shot. Keep the club in an upright position on the backswing, which will let the ball travel in a straight line.

If you have to hook the ball around a tree, you have to use a closed stance. Also, make sure the V's are pointed toward your right shoulder. This will cause automatic pronation as your hands come into the hitting area. Play the ball in the middle of your stance and be sure to keep your body down as you hit through the shot.

It's almost the opposite when you're trying to slice around an obstacle. Use an open stance, address the ball with a slightly open clubface, and keep the V's pointing toward your chin. Play the ball just a little left of center. Also, keep the club in an upright position on your backswing as this will cause you to cut across the ball, thus giving it a slice spin.

When you're playing the ball out of a divot hole or off the bare ground, you use an abrupt, descending blow and hit the bottom portion of the ball cleanly. On this shot *do not* swing as fast as you normally would. And use a longer club than usual so you can compensate for the restricted lie.

Speaking of trouble shots, there are the two rascals that make the life of the high-handicapper a nightmare—only this time he's directly responsible. These are the shank and the sky shot. We've touched on it in an earlier chapter, but now we're going into an in-depth study of the chip and the sky shot.

Shanking is regarded as the most mysterious of all golf shots. This is the shot that abruptly flies off the clubhead at right angles to the target line. And it strikes without a bit of warning. A player can be in the middle of a terrific round, and suddenly, for no apparent reason, the ball squirts to the right as he stands there flabbergasted.

At this point the golfer loses all his confidence and hits the panic button. Until he hit the shank, the thought of it never entered his mind. But from that point on, every time he picks out a short iron (these are the clubs most likely to produce the shank) he's thinking about the shank. With this fear in mind, it is probable that the shanker will either pull the next shot or shank again.

If the player learns what causes shanking, he need never fear it. Once he learns what part of the club has hit the ball and what fault in his swing needs to be corrected, the problem should never bother him again. The shank occurs when the ball is struck by the nozzle, or neck, of the shaft instead of the clubhead. The face of the clubhead never touched the ball, and you can prove it by eyeing the white mark on the neck of the shaft.

The shot is caused by *not* turning on the backswing. As you begin the downswing, you start down with the right shoulder and arms, pushing the club outside the line of flight. And the shank results.

The first step in correcting this ailment is to distribute your weight evenly over the arches of both feet. Make sure the left arm is straight and extended away from your body. Since one of the main causes of the shank is a strong right side, you have to create a weaker position for this culprit. Have your right arm relaxed and closer to the body and lower than your left arm.

Begin the take-away with the left shoulder taking the club straight back, and make sure you've got a good pivot. Now, this next move is the critical one in correcting shanking. MAKE SURE YOU DO NOT INITIATE THE DOWNSWING WITH YOUR HANDS AND RIGHT SHOULDER! Make the hips move laterally toward the left. This action will give the correct inside-out swing and delay the power of the hands in the hitting area.

Remember, the swing that produces the shank is so far to the outside of the arc that you took the club back with that there is absolutely no way you can strike the ball with the clubface. The

"BURIED"

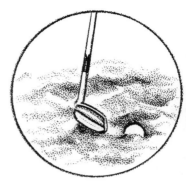

... OFF RIGHT HEEL ...

... CLUB UPRIGHT ...

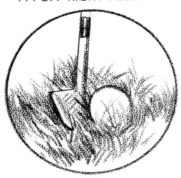

... CLOSER LOOK ...

AND WITH THE WOODS

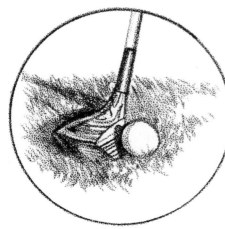

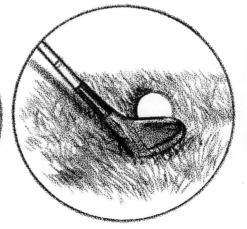

... THESE ARE IDEAL LIES TO BE PLAYED WITH WOODS.

SOMETIMES A "RIGHTY"
HAS TO GO "LEFTY"

only part of the club that will make contact is the neck of the club.

If you're having problems along these lines, try consciously to think about hitting the ball with the toe of your club instead of the middle of the clubface. Bring the club down inside the arc of your backswing; this will enable you to hit the ball more on the toe than on the sweet spot. Of course, after you've gotten over the fear of the shank you can go back to swinging away as you usually do. The big item here is *not* to panic. Stay calm and cool and remember what causes the shank and how you're going to correct it and you'll have no problem.

Skying, although disconcerting, is less serious and more easily corrected than the shank. This is the shot that soars high and doesn't go far, and you'll usually find a big divot after you've completed the shot. Of course, sometimes skying occurs off the tee.

In a sky shot contact is made with most of the clubface below the center of the ball. The player is staying too long on his right side. This causes him to hit the ball too soon. And on the downswing the hands and arms are moving before proper weight distribution has been made. The clubhead is then traveling at a sharp angle, which results in hitting the ground and the ball at the same time. The ground slows up the clubhead speed, the club goes under the ball, and you may find a white mark on the top of your clubface for the effort.

TROUBLE SHOTS **95**

To correct this skying problem, make sure you construct a swing that will bring the clubhead along the proper path parallel to the ground. When you address the ball, make sure your weight is mostly on the left side. The farther the shot, the more weight on the left side.

Bring the club back slowly as you transfer your weight from the left side to the right. Then, when you're at the top of your backswing, get the feeling that you're going to move the entire left side of your body by pulling with your left shoulder, or side, clearing the way for the right side to come into the swing. Most players want to hit the ball with their hands. They don't understand that it's the lower part of the body that supplies the power.

Skying is more frequent when you're hitting a tee shot. It could be that you're teeing the ball too high. And, you could be dipping the right shoulder. But just remember, keep the head steady and the arc on the downswing the same as on the backswing, and you'll soon work yourself out of this trouble shot.

As I've said many times before—and I'm going to keep on saying it throughout this book—there is absolutely no substitute for practice. If you want to improve your game—and I'm sure you do, or you wouldn't be reading this—you have to practice this shot and that shot—in fact, all the shots. And when you get finished with the regular tee practice, hit a few balls out of the rough. Then hit some out of the sand. This is the only way you're going to whip your game into shape so you'll be able to play with the scratch and low-handicap players.

17 PRACTICE AND REVIEW

I keep harping on practice, so what say we go down to the practice tee and review what we've covered to date.

A reminder: A good warming exercise when you reach the practice area is simply to swing a club, first slowly, then progressively harder. Get a firm grip on the club, take a comfortable stance, and swing the club back and forth. Again, swing easily at first and then progress into the power swing as you go along. It will surprise you how you can loosen your muscles until you feel you want to hit that ball a mile.

The first club to start with is the pitching wedge. When I use the wedge, I have my feet fairly close together and play the ball off my right heel. My hands are ahead of the ball and the club at point of address. The swing is always the same—straight back, straight through. The take-away is slow and deliberate, and the hips initiate the swing.

Remember, this short pitch is the framework of your entire game. If you are basically right here, you will be basically right as you go up the scale to your driver. I concentrate on getting my hands and arms going to the target. This thought helps me make the sure shot and the correct follow-through. On this short shot make sure your wrists and arms remain rigid. This is strictly a shoulder swing.

After hitting seven or eight wedge shots, I go into the short irons (nine, eight, and seven). The main thought here is accuracy rather than distance. With the short, elevated clubs you're going for the pin, not the green. I use the open stance with the ball played more to the center, but not quite, at the point of address. This open stance (with the left foot drawn back about 2 inches) restricts my shoulder swing going back and assures me of a more accurate shot.

Good rhythm is essential with these short irons. Good rhythm with the short clubs carries over to good timing with the longer, less lofted clubs. I never force the shot with these short irons. I just try to swing easily with a smooth tempo and concentrate on throwing my arms out toward the target.

Now we go to the midirons (six, five, and four). Here the plan definitely changes from an open stance to a square stance. The feet are wider apart, and the ball is played in the middle of the stance. The reason for the square stance with these midirons is that you need a bigger turn of the shoulders and hips. This stance enables me to get the full turn simply because I'm using a longer club.

I'm not going to take the club back much farther than I did with my short irons. Maybe about three-quarters of the backswing I use on my long irons and driver. Of course, the more shoulder turn, the more distance. But at the same time I have the club in complete control of the left hand. As I hit these middle-distance shots (about 125 to 150 yards), I make sure that my left shoulder passes under my chin on the backswing and that at the top of the backswing my left shoulder is pointing right at the ball.

Let me reiterate that the hands are working the same as in the higher lofted clubs—always ahead of the ball at point of address and until you make contact. Also, as in all shots, your eyes are at the back, or hitting point, of the ball. And don't forget the follow-through.

Hitting the long irons (three and two) is just like hitting the woods. With a long iron you're hitting the ball off your left heel, your stance has widened to the point where your feet are spaced just as wide as your shoulders, and you're taking the full turn of the shoulders and hips. You're no longer going for the pin; you're going for the middle of the green. Of course, by now you're hitting the ball from 175 to 210 yards, and the margin for error has greatly increased. Don't forget the grip. Firm, but still not with a life-or-death pressure.

Now we come to the real fun part of the game—hitting the woods. I know I'm small and like to show off with 300-yard drives —to me this is the sweet part of the game. First we'll start off with the fairway woods (five, four, and three). I say five, four, and three because these are the woods I carry in my bag.

I use the same swing as I used on the long irons except that now I am coming through the hitting area much faster and with more power. This speed must come both from your hands and from your legs because this is where you get your increased distance. Also, as with the shorter clubs, make sure that the swing is initiated by the turning of the hips.

When I get to the driver, I am completely loose and really pour it on. When I use the driver I try to save my club speed for just before I hit the ball. In other words, I don't uncock my wrists until just before I unload on the ball. For this club, more than any other, you must have good balance and fast hand and arm action through the hitting area. Your right arm is tucked in close to the body, and the left arm is fully extended at point of contact.

Now I'm ready for the course. But first I'm going to go to the practice trap and hit a few sand shots. First test the sand for

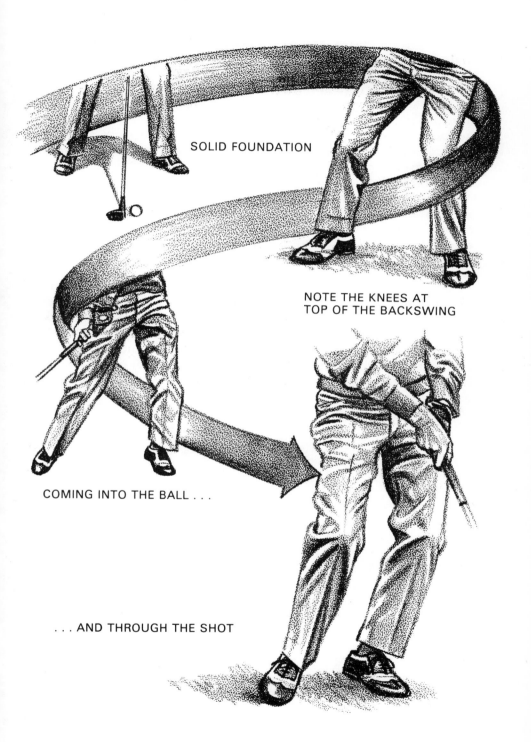

SOLID FOUNDATION

NOTE THE KNEES AT
TOP OF THE BACKSWING

COMING INTO THE BALL . . .

. . . AND THROUGH THE SHOT

texture—soft, dense, wet. You do this by walking in it. Then you dig in, get anchored. You're using the open stance, practically facing the target. And this is one shot in which you're not looking at the back of the ball; you're looking at a spot about an inch behind the ball, depending on the density of the sand.

I don't crowd the ball, and I usually play it off my left ankle. And I always make sure that I swing through the shot. There is absolutely no babying this shot—you have to cut through the sand. If you have a buried lie, close the clubface. As you practice this explosion shot, you'll find that you'll be able to adjust to the different distances.

A couple of short shots out of the high grass around the practice green and we'll be ready to go. You play these shots mostly with the higher lofted clubs, but on occasion you'll find that a seven or even a six iron will do the job better. Again, it's the club that's the most comfortable that handles the shot. You don't break the wrists. This is strictly a shoulder maneuver.

Oh, yes, the putting green. Putting is the only part of the game of golf where each man is on his own. Sure, I can tell you what to look for and how to read the greens, but in the end it's strictly a solo act between you and that little putter you hold in your hand.

In the next chapters we're going into the more complicated part of the game—such things as psyching yourself, your diet, exercising. We're going to have you in the 70s before you know it.

18 THE THINKING MAN'S GAME

Golf is a thinking man's game. You can have all the shots in the bag, but if you don't know what to do with them, you've got troubles. In this chapter we'll go into what a good golfer is thinking about as he surveys a golf course.

They call them "two o'clock hitters" in baseball. In golf they say they left their game on the practice tee. We're talking about the sweet swinger during practice shots who folds like an accordion during championship play. At any rate, here are some tips on how to improve your game when you're under pressure.

Relaxation is the key to pressure golf. When our practicing sweet swinger walks on the No. 1 tee, his mental outlook does an about-face. On the range or on the practice green he was mentally relaxed. He was in complete control of his muscles. Now, when he goes into competition, he has three opponents—the other players, Old Man Par, and mostly himself. He'll now be trying so hard that he'll lose most of his technical skill that has taken so long to develop.

Here's a situation that's familiar to most of us. This fellow plays to about a ten handicap under friendly competition. He enters the club championship tournament and suddenly can't hit the ground with his hat. Again, like the sweet swinger, our boy has lost control of his muscles under pressure.

How do you handle the situation if you always collapse in competitive play? Here are a few tips that may help if you find yourself falling into this category. They are comparatively simple but they do require a certain amount of insight into what type of game you play.

The player standing on the first tee, usually without even the benefit of taking any practice-tee time, must realize that he's going to make some bad shots during the eighteen holes to come. Every shot certainly isn't going to come off as he expected to play it. He also is going to blow some putts that he normally should make. He probably will three-putt a couple or three greens. If he will just realize this, he will be much better prepared mentally to accept things as they are.

All of this may seem to be thinking negatively, but this isn't the case so far as the high-handicapper is concerned. In fact, thinking as we suggested should relax our man and put him in a more favorable frame of mind. With this approach he will realize that *no* player is able to hit every shot just the way he plans it. So he must forget the bad shots and the bad holes and look forward to the next one.

While realizing that there will be bad shots and bad holes, the 15-handicapper must also realize that there'll be times when he's not going to score as well or below his average. And during any round there will be times when he's going to come up with exceptional shots. This is especially true around the greens where a chip shot may go in or he may sink two or three long putts. In other words, he must accept the good with the bad and *not* just remember the bad shots and expect the good.

There's another mental situation that the average weekender must accept if he is going to be able to handle the game of golf. As he plays his once-a-week match, he's going to run into problems that call for a variety of shots. This, of course, will present problems that the average player can't handle. So, instead of becoming frustrated, he must realize that the pro or low-handicapper plays much more golf than he does and is much better equipped to handle these situations.

There's also the problem of selection of clubs. The weekend golfer will use his driver about fourteen times in a round and his putter between thirty and thirty-eight times. He may use his three iron only once in the entire eighteen holes. So how can he possibly expect to use the three iron with any degree of authority when he uses it only once or twice a week?

The touring pro, on the other hand, hits every club in his bag many times a week—if not in actual play, at least off the practice tee for the time when he'll need it under pressure conditions. But even the pros goof shots. As Ben Hogan once said: "I hit only four or five shots a round just the way I want to." The weekend player must realize this before he hits his first ball off the first tee.

Weather is another factor that must be considered by the once-a-week player. Say he's a 90 shooter, and when he shows up for the Saturday game, the weather has turned against him and is cold and drizzly and the wind is blowing. But he and his buddies are determined to play the match. Before he even hits his first ball he must realize that his score is going to soar close to the 100 figure for the eighteen holes. This is true not only for the amateur but for the pro as well. Weather conditions always affect the play of everyone.

Now we come into the territory of planning your round. The serious golfer should become aware of all problems presented by a course, hole by hole. This includes knowing the distances to all bunkers, water hazards, and obstacles between the tee and the amateur's average drive and between the drive and the green.

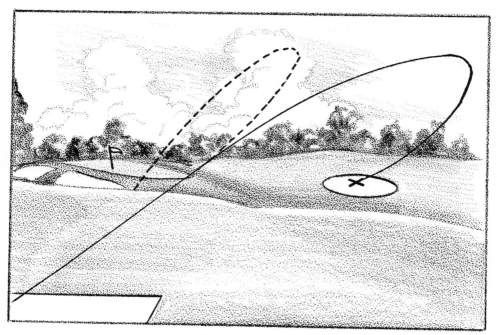

I HAVE A DEFINITE PLAN FOR EVERY TEE SHOT. ON THIS HOLE THERE
ARE BUNKERS ON THE LEFT, SO, NATURALLY, I SHOOT TO THE RIGHT.
SURE, THE DOTTED LINE SHOWS THE SHORTEST WAY, BUT IN THIS
CASE THE BEST SHOT IS THE SOLID LINE.

A good way to plan a round is to pace off distances from land-
marks on the course to the center of each green. These marks can
include such things as trees, bushes, water-sprinkler heads, and
posts. Knowing exact distances, naturally, is an asset in making
the correct club selection. And it's also nice to know about pin
placements. In playing to larger greens you may elect to use more
club than is usually called for.

Naturally, distances mean little if you don't know how far you
can hit your club. And you can't go by another player's choice. The
stronger player, of course, will use less club than the weaker
player. You'll just have to find out how far you hit the various
clubs by measuring your shots on the practice tee. I know this
seems like a lot of bother, but if you want to be a better golfer, you
have to find out.

When you reach the first tee, begin planning. Study the fairway
and adjacent areas for trouble spots. Estimate the distance to the
hazards, or the one most likely to affect your shot, and then choose
a club that will logically permit you to shoot around trouble.

An example: If you see a bunker on one side of the fairway and you figure your drive will reach it, shoot for the other side of the fairway. Or take a lesser club and shoot short of the trouble. Another helpful hint: Tee up your ball on the trouble side where you'll have more room to maneuver. Strangely enough, most high-handicappers do just the opposite. They tee up the ball farthest from the trouble spot, and this narrows the fairway and directs the ball to the trouble.

Another cheerful earful: DON'T TAKE CHANCES that might cost you strokes. If there's a bunker between you and the green, play short and try to wedge it close on your next shot. Many a player has won money and prestige by NOT going for the green when there's a possibility of landing in a trouble spot on the way.

On par-three holes tee up the ball. That old saw about *not* teeing up an iron is nonsense. If you'll notice the touring pros, you'll see that they tee up every tee shot. However, the ball should be teed just high enough to create a good lie. This lets you take the usual divot and get backspin on the ball if the shot requires backspin.

In heavy rough don't press the panic button. Make your first order of business *escape.* It's much better to get out of the rough first and then go about getting to the green than to try to make it all the way and land in the rough again just a few yards ahead of your shot. Also don't get greedy when you have to play over a

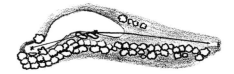

THIS HOLE IS 385 YARDS LONG. YOU CAN'T
HIT THE BIG TEE SHOT TO THE RIGHT BECAUSE
OF A BIG TREE THAT GUARDS THE GREEN. SO
THE BEST WAY TO PLAY THIS HOLE IS TO HIT
SHORT OF THE FAIRWAY TRAP ON THE LEFT SIDE.

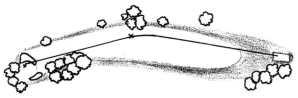

THIS HOLE IS 425 YARDS WITH HUGE TREES
GUARDING THE GREEN ON THE LEFT. YOU HAVE
TO HIT THE BOMB HERE, AND TO THE RIGHT SO
YOU'LL HAVE AN OPEN SHOT TO THE GREEN.

bunker to reach a green and the pin is cut close to the fringe closest to you. Instead of finessing the shot and landing in the bunker first make sure you reach the green. It's much easier to sink a long putt than to hit an explosion shot into the cup.

Plan ahead on every shot. When you start walking down the fairway after you hit off the tee, study the advantages of this or that shot. Look for the hazards and bend your next shot away from the trouble areas. Then, after you have your course of action set firmly in your mind, concentrate on the mechanics of pulling off the shot. Of course, you can think too much. If you become obsessed with the hazards on the course and have to check and recheck your course of action, you're thinking negatively. And this creates fear and builds tension so you won't be able to hit any kind of shot with authority.

Don't ever doubt that you can make the shot. Think positively. After you've made up your mind, ignore the trouble and concentrate on pleasant things . . . like a long, straight shot to the pin. Think of these things and then execute the shot in a smooth rhythmical way.

Another thing, don't consciously press on long holes. Never look at the distant green. Instead, just think that you're playing a series of three par-three holes. Select a target for your tee shot and play to it. Then do the same for your second shot and execute it. I think more wood shots have been flubbed on long par fives than in any other situation. The reason being that the amateur thinks the green is so remote that he forgets he can reach it by hitting just one shot at a time.

Don't try for distance out of a trap. Leave this to the pros. Your shot is to get the ball back into play. Use a lofted club and expect to hit short. Play the ball to the right of your target because the clubface will close when you're hitting through sand.

Be sure to take wind and weather into consideration. If you have a following wind, use a lesser club. Use a longer club if you're hitting into a wind. Long approach shots out of the rough should be hit harder than fairway shots.

Warm hands are most important in cold weather, and dry hands are most important in wet weather. I always make it a point to keep the palms of both hands covered.

The high-handicapper can enjoy any round of golf he plays *if* he takes into consideration the things he can expect of himself. First he must realize that the game of golf is a fun game. He must remember that he can't hit every shot on the sweet spot or expect the shot to go to the target every time. He's not playing the game for a living. No matter what you shoot, you should play golf for its great value as a contest for gentlemen and ladies. And it's played in the finest possible setting—the great outdoors.

19 THE PAR THREES

How many times have you stood on a par-three hole, thrown grass into the air to measure the wind, and said to yourself: "I wonder what club to use on this one"? Well, I can't tell you exactly, but I can give you a few tips that might help you the next time you're wondering.

First, say you're shooting for an elevated green. On this one, depending on height, you'll have to use at least one club longer, maybe two. The reason for this is that it's all carry, and you're going to have to get more power into your shot so it will carry that extra distance that the elevation makes for.

Other factors you have to take into consideration on all par threes are wind, the condition of the green, the tilt of the green, and pin placement. Also, consider whether you want to hit a high, floating shot that needs to hold or a line-drive type that will land in front of the green and roll on toward the pin. The condition of the course will dictate your decision in these cases.

Don't try to squeeze more distance from a shot than your normal swing would give you, especially on a par three. A high-handicapper often goes in for this faulty thinking: If the other guy hits a five iron, I can hit a five iron. Or maybe I'll show him how powerful I am by hitting a six. This is false pride and you're bound to end up behind the eight ball. Another thing about pressing a shot: You'll inevitably pull it. One thing for sure, you're not going to have the control on a pressed shot that you do on one in which you use your normal swing and follow-through.

As I mentioned in the previous chapter, you should always tee the ball up on a par three. When the rules give you a break, take advantage of it. Of course, you won't want to tee up too high—just as high as a ball would be sitting on a perfectly manicured fairway. If you tee the ball too high, you're going to be looking at a "rain-maker," and if you tee it too low you may end up sculling the shot.

There are two ways to play a two-level or built-up green (one in which the apron is lower than the putting surface). If the pin is far enough back, you'll want to use a high, floating shot, one that grabs when it hits. If the pin is fairly close, you'll have to run the ball onto the green. The run-up shot is one of the most treasured in the bag of the shooting pros, and its value should be recognized by the average player. Play this shot just as you would a long chip —ball off the right toe, wrist break from the start of the backswing, and a firm, crisp downswing.

Wind shots on par threes are always a problem. The tournament player is able to make a lot of swing compensations that the 18-handicapper isn't able to do. So I recommend that you change your target, depending on the direction of the breeze. If you're hitting into the wind, use more club, less if you're going with the wind. And position the ball as to your usual stance, either forward or back.

A real par-three fooler is one protected by a grove of trees. When you're standing on the tee, the wind is whipping, and you just naturally feel that this is the way the wind is blowing all the way to the green. Not so! First, look at that pin flag and see how it's fluttering. Then look at the top of the trees and see how they're moving. Finally, look for movement in the leaves in the middle of the trees.

On a crosswind you have to remember that it will knock off just about one club length's worth of distance, just about like a headwind. So you'll have to use the next longer club when the wind is blowing either from the right or from the left. As I said in the preceding chapter, golf is a thinking man's game and should be played as such.

Also in a preceeding chapter we discussed how to slice and how to draw a golf ball. This comes in handy for pin placements on these par threes. Say you have a long, narrow green that bends to the left and the pin is at the back in the left-hand corner. This is an ideal spot for the draw shot—one that starts out to the right and comes back to hit on the front of the green; then, since the spin on the ball is from right to left, the ball will roll that way and follow the contour of the green to the pin. Just the opposite is true if the pin is on the right side of a green that bends from left to right. This, of course, calls for a controlled slice.

Both shots have many advantages, including maneuvering around bunkers, trees, water, and other obstacles that are between the player and the pin. If you have control of these draws and slices, you'll never have to wonder if your ball is going too far or going to plop short into a yawning bunker.

A short review on how to play these shots: On the draw, the left foot is an inch or two in front of the right foot according to the flight line. You make sure you use the inside-out swing with the full follow-through. On the slice shot, your left foot is an inch or two in back of the right foot and the swing is more or less from the outside-in. Of course, the position of the feet in both cases dictates the swing. Also, the grip comes into play here. (See illustration.)

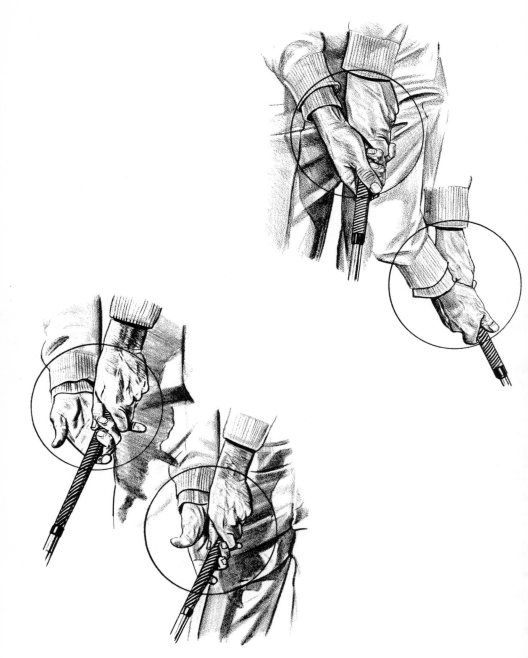

HOOK GRIP
WITH THE RIGHT HAND IN BACK OF THE CLUB AND THE V'S POINTING
TOWARD THE RIGHT SHOULDER

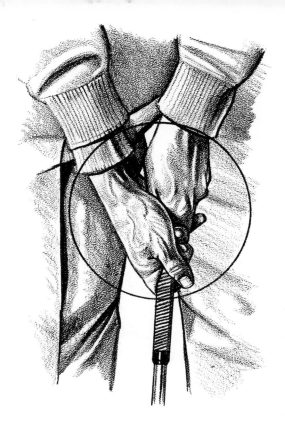

HOOK

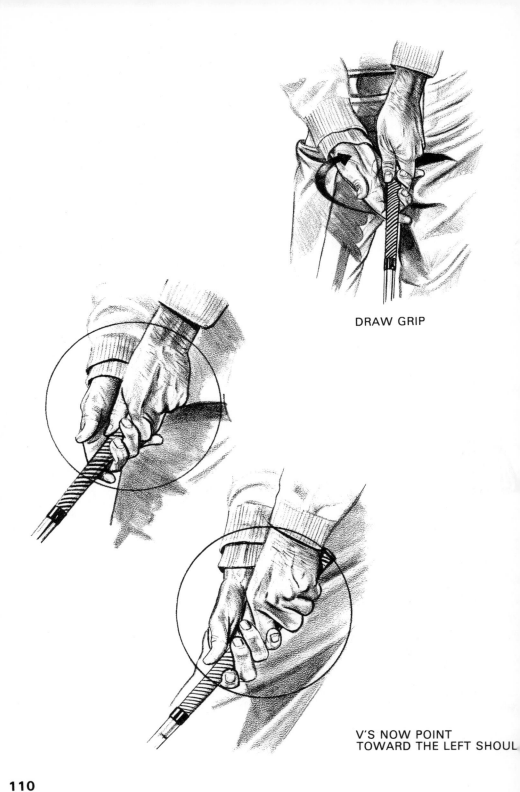

DRAW GRIP

V'S NOW POINT
TOWARD THE LEFT SHOUL

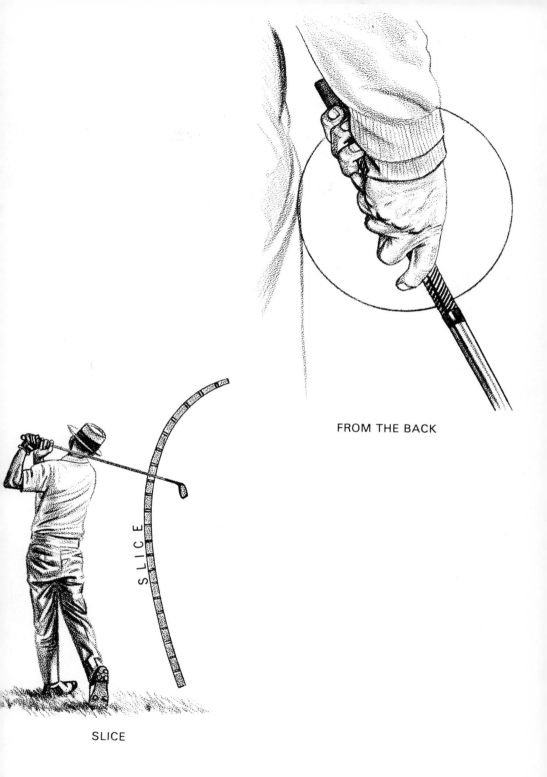

FROM THE BACK

SLICE

I know all of you have run into a green that is tipped away from the player. This poses a real problem, especially on par threes. You don't know whether to hit the ball high and let it float into the green when it might not hold. Or to hit a low shot that lands in front and rolls on.

First, you have to examine the terrain. If the green has bunkers or water in front of it, then, quite naturally, you're going to have to float the ball. If, however, there's no trouble between tee and green, I would recommend a roll-on shot. On this type of tilted green you're going to have to hit the ball higher than usual. This gives you more bite, and the ball will hold better. Say you're undecided between a two and a three iron. In this case I would suggest you'd better use a five wood. That way you have more power to get the ball higher. Also, tee the ball higher than usual. Remember the higher and longer you can keep the ball in the air the more bite you're going to have on the green.

Now, say the green is tilted toward you. In this case you don't want much backspin on the ball, as that would make it back off the green. You'll therefore want to use a more direct line on your shot because the tilt of the green will give the ball the amount of bite you'll need to hold the shot. Also, this calls for a lower tee-up position for your ball.

In the next chapter we're going into the playing of the par fours and fives. I want to impress upon you the need for practice. But if you're having trouble with any of the shots outlined in this book, go to your local professional. He'll probably straighten you out in a hurry.

20 THE PAR FOURS AND FIVES

Terrain and the study of same are the key to par-four and par-five holes. You have to know where the trouble spots are, the distance you can hit your shots, and the best possible approach to each green.

The long par four is like a short par five to the high-handicapper and should be played as such. Nothing is more disheartening than to take a double or triple bogey on a hole that you figured at least to bogey. One of the biggest mistakes for the weekender is to go all-out with the driver, hoping for a short iron to the green. If you keep in mind that a three wood and a five iron are the same as a driver and a seven iron, you'll have much more peace of mind going into the hole.

One of the most important parts of playing any hole is thinking about your second shot even before you've hit off the tee. Most high-handicappers step up on the tee without even thinking about what they're going to do with that second shot. You have to take into consideration the whole hole, and playing it that way instead of doing it by bits and pieces is the only sure solution.

Let's take a medium-length par four with a slight dogleg right that is heavily bunkered along the left side from about 160 yards to the green. Also, the green is trapped on the left side only. Since all the trouble is on the left side, there's an obvious advantage to hitting the tee shot down the right side of the fairway. For the average player a three wood or a two iron off the tee would be the right club selection, depending on how he used each club.

If the hole was a long one with the same hazard positions, it would be wise to play for a bogey. In this case you'd use a driver off the tee, since you couldn't reach any trouble with a long shot. Another thing to remember is *not* to shoot for the pin on your second shot.

Let's take another for-instance: another dogleg left, bunkered on both sides at the turn, trees on the right from tee to green and with a huge bunker in front of the green. To par this hole in the accepted manner, you have to hit the middle of the fairway between the bunkers with your drive. At this point it would be much easier for the high-handicapper to play short of the fairway bunkers, lay up short to the green bunker, and then chip for the flag.

Doglegs pose big problems for the average player; he tends to

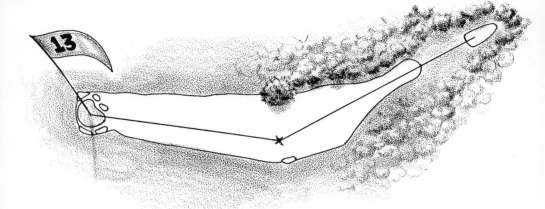

FIRESTONE COUNTRY CLUB
PAR FOUR, THIRTEENTH HOLE
460 YARDS

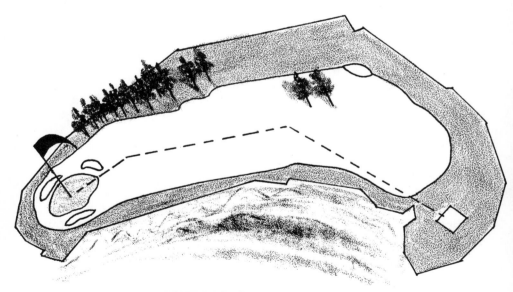

PEBBLE BEACH
DEL MONTE LODGE, CALIFORNIA
PAR FIVE, EIGHTEENTH HOLE
540 YARDS

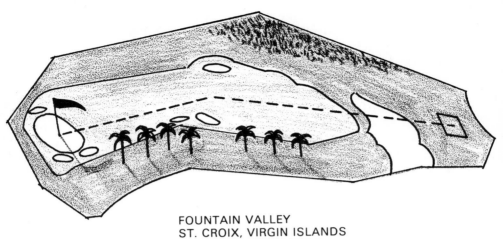

FOUNTAIN VALLEY
ST. CROIX, VIRGIN ISLANDS
PAR FOUR, NINTH HOLE
470 YARDS

EL CONQUISTADOR
LAS CROABAS, PUERTO RICO
PAR FOUR, THIRD HOLE
420 YARDS

try to play these holes like a pro—cutting the corners. However, it is much wiser to play away from the bend where the green opens up for a clear shot. On the other hand, the dogleg side of the fairway is often blocked by additional trouble near the green.

Short par fours—250 to 325 yarders—are especially dangerous. You can be assured that the design of the hole is such that there's trouble awaiting your drive. When a hole looks easy by distance, it's usually tougher by hazards. The same applies to the short par fives.

On par-five holes the most important shot isn't your driver; it's your second shot. This applies not only to the weekend golfer but to the professional as well. Most pros and low-handicap players look upon par fives as birdie country and try to make the green in two shots. But the high-handicapper should be content to make the green in three or even four shots on the longer fives.

The second shot should put the good player on or near the green. Players who don't make a living from the game should play the second shot for position, setting up a sure shot to the green or a spot right in front of it. If the hole is that long, a good chip and one putt will take care of the par.

Here's a par five to work on. This one won't be too long but will have trouble in the form of a lake to the left, which runs from halfway down the fairway to the green. There are bunkers and trees to the right. The long hitter, if he stays in the right fairway, can drive past the trouble on the right and thus set up a five- or six-iron shot to the green. Thus he's home free with a bird.

Shorter hitters have a choice: They can live dangerously or safely. A drive of about 200 yards will carry to the narrow part of the fairway. However, if the drive isn't straight, it could catch the trees or the bunker on the right or the lake on the left. So the shot off the tee (if you're playing it safe) should be made with a two or three iron so that it will carry about 175 yards. The second shot also should be played with an iron or a five wood, whichever you handle better. Of course, you're not within green range, so don't try to stretch the shot. Then a wedge to the green will get you into position for a sure par, and if you get lucky, you may be close enough to make the bird.

Now, for a long par five. This doglegs left with water all along the left side and trees and bunkers on the right side. The long hitter can get past the trees and bunkers on the right but still cannot reach the green on the second shot. Long hitters play this hole as strictly a par five. But weekenders who hit the shorter ball are going to have problems. They should play this hole as a par six.

The safe way is to drive off the tee with a fairway wood or long iron. This will enable you to have more accuracy, which is needed to stay out of the water on the left. It will leave you plenty of room for the second shot, which should carry midway between tee and green. The third shot is then played again for the middle of the fairway. Of course, these three shots have to be straight. The fourth shot, since it's into the narrow part of the fairway in front of the green, should be cozied up to the front of the green. A short pitch will get you home, and two putts will assure the bogey.

On most par fives there's plenty of room for the drive, but it's the second shot that gets you into trouble. Trouble on most holes comes with the second shot to the green as most fairways narrow and are plastered with bunkers, trees, and water. So the safe way to play all these holes is to think about it first and hit second. A long second shot won't do the trick if you find trouble. A safe, straight shot is best under all conditions.

21 THAT BAD LEFT ARM

In the preceding chapter we talked about accuracy on the par fours and fives; if you don't have that accuracy, especially on the second shot, you might as well forget about lowering your score. One of the most important and most discussed elements of your swing, and one that deals with accuracy, is the left arm. How many times on the golf course have you heard one high-handicapper admonish another that his left arm was crooked?

Well, in this chapter I'm going to blow the lid off all those amateur instructors who preach that the left arm should be rigidly straight at all times. I'm going to tell you that not only the left arm should be straight but the right one as well. Of course, I'm not going to sell the theory that both should be straight at all times. But at point of impact BOTH ARMS SHOULD BE FULLY EXTENDED!

It is generally agreed that a fully extended left arm, along with a steady head throughout the backswing, assures the desired downswing and a complete follow-through. The less bend at the elbow, the less adjustment you'll have to make with the arms going into point of impact.

It is also agreed that the desired straight left arm can be achieved only if you start with it straight at the address point. And if you can continue to hold the line to completion, you're bound to get a good shot.

However, there are many top pros on the tournament circuit who are far from perfect with the left-arm bit. One of these is Sam Snead, the picture swinger. If you watch Sam, you'll note that at the top of his backswing there's a slight bend in the left elbow. However, Sam will have the left arm straight just after starting his downswing, and it will stay straight until he has completed his swing.

This doesn't mean that bending the left elbow should be condoned. Anybody who's serious about lowering his score should always be aware of the left arm and of the fact that it should be kept as straight as possible. The straight left arm is the foundation of a consistent, simplified swing. But we must recognize that, when we reach for the best possible swing arc, the clubhead weight tends to bend the elbow a few degrees even in the best of golfers.

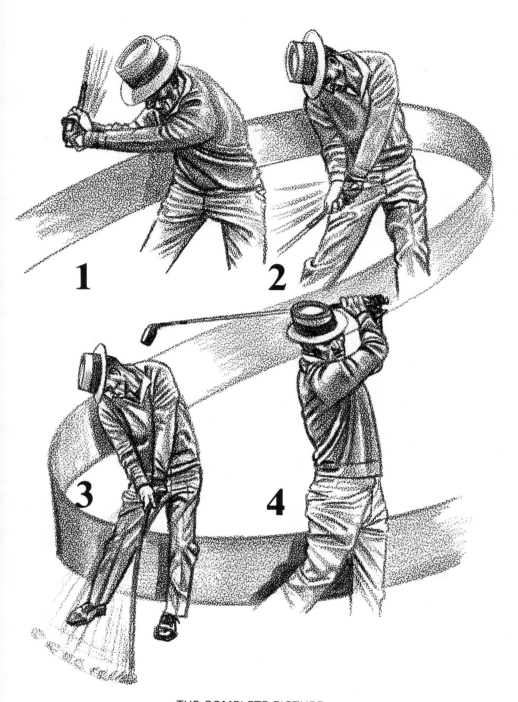

THE COMPLETE PICTURE

It's just logical that the farther back the clubhead goes, the more chance you have of bending the elbow. And since we're always reaching for more distance, it's only natural that we take the club back as far as possible on our backswing.

The conclusion reached among the pros is that a slight bend in the left elbow at the top of the backswing is probably no more disastrous than lifting the club at take-away, or a slight head sway, or a slight flying of the right elbow, or, for that matter, any movement that has to be corrected as you bring the club down and into the ball at point of impact.

As everyone knows, the simpler the swing, the easier it is to correct any maladjustments the player has to make. In other words, the fewer moves you have to make when hitting the golf ball, the more practical the swing. The most serious consequence of any of the malpractices we mortals engage in on the golf course, compensating adjustments tend to complicate the entire operation of the swing.

And anything that complicates the swing introduces more probability of error. And, since we all work on our errors, it takes more practice to ease these mistakes. All of which suggests that the professional, who plays every day, can compensate for any hitch in his swing, while the weekend player has to struggle along in the 90s.

Another misnomer so far as the left arm is concerned is the word "stiff." As you know, "stiff" connotes no movement. And with no movement there's no way to hit the golf ball. The proper term for keeping the left arm in its desired position is "extended." "Fully extended" says it all without confusing the issue. And since "fully extended," to me isn't the same as "fully extended," to you, each player should strive for full extension within his own physical makeup.

About the straight right arm: As all golfers who have studied the game know, there is a time in your swing when your right arm has to be as straight as your left arm. This occurs at point of impact and carries through almost to the completion of your follow-through. Of course, this is minor compared with the left arm, since the right will just follow the left's lead, or should.

Now, let's get back to the fully extended left arm and clear up something that may have become contorted in the telling. I don't say it's right to bend the elbow at the top of the swing even though Sam Snead does it. But if you're going to bend the left elbow at all, it *has* to be at the top of the backswing.

If your elbow is fully extended at point of address, it should be kept fully extended at least until just before the top of the backswing. Bending the left elbow as part of lifting the club to get it over your head is a no-no, contrary to every law of golf in the swinging of the club.

However, *if* you must bend at the top of your swing, keep it to a minimum. Remember, the more bend going back the more adjustment to be made during the downswing. Fortunately, this adjustment requires no special thought or effort to execute so long as the player keeps his head behind the shot and reaches full extension of both arms at impact.

Wrapping it up: If you bend going back, it's all right so long as you're fully extended coming down. And, if you take a 45-degree hip turn and at least an 85-per-cent shoulder turn, you're going to find it much easier to keep that left arm fully extended all the way.

22 TEAM PLAY

I think we all know that golf is an individual effort. You're out there all alone with nobody to blame except yourself if anything goes wrong. But once in a while you'll run into team play, as we professionals do in, say, the Ryder Cup Matches.

This puts you into another phase of the game. According to what rules you're using, of course, in most team play you're permitted to help your partners. As you know, in all PGA tournaments when you're out there on your own, you can't ask any other player what club he used, or about distances, or anything like that. But team play is different.

Let's say we're playing in the Columbia Broadcasting System (CBS) doubles tournament at Firestone Country Club. Now, my partner gets on the green in two and is farther away from the hole but in a direct line with my ball. I'm lying three and can only par this par-four hole. He, on the other hand, can get us a birdie. So I'll putt first so he can see the line that my ball will travel in.

This is a two-fold operation on our part. If I make my putt, he can charge for his bird. If I miss, he can more or less lag toward the hole so he has a sure par.

Along these same lines, say your opponents have the same situation and you *don't* want the closer player to show his partner the line. All you have to do in this case is to give the putt, and he is forced to take it under the rules we play by. I'll tell you a little incident that happened in the 1973 Ryder Cup Matches in Scotland. We were captained by Jackie Burke, who, incidentally, is one of the fine veterans of the game. Well, I wasn't feeling too well after the first two individual rounds, so I went to Burke and told him that I felt I wouldn't be doing the team any good if I played the next day. So he played Homero Blancas, who was supposed to sit out this particular round.

I thought I could be of some help if I followed Lee Trevino and Blancas around the course; as you know, both are Latinos, the same as I. I kidded with them and helped them on distances as best I could. As it turned out, this was one of the wisest decisions I ever made. Trevino and Blancas played super golf and won their match easily.

Yes, team play can be challenging and interesting and especially a lot of fun. And that's what we're looking for—challenges, interest, and entertainment. It's what makes the world go around, and I'm sure glad I've had my share of it all in my lifetime.

23 KEEPING IN SHAPE

Back in Walter Hagen's day, the nineteenth hole was generally accepted as a scene for fun and games, frivolity and the long quaff. But this has changed. If a pro wants to walk to the pay window on Sundays, he has to stay in shape. I know it's a little different with the high-handicapper, but he, too, could take some tips from the guys who travel from course to course in search of gold.

One big factor in today's game that wasn't here a couple of decades ago is the big, strong youngster who hits the ball a mile with accuracy and is able to play all day without tiring. As in all sports, performers today are bigger and stronger, and if we little guys want to stay in the hunt, we've got to be ready at all times.

A for-instance in my case. Near the end of the 1960s I went into a bad slump. I couldn't hit my way out of a paper sack; furthermore, I couldn't have cared less. In other words, I had become lazy. During my practice rounds at my home course in Puerto Rico, I was even riding a cart.

Then one day in 1971 I got the shock of my lifetime. I was dropped off the selected list. That meant I'd have to qualify for every tournament I entered. This was a real come-down for me since I'd been one of the fair-haired boys for a long time. Sure, I hadn't been winning, but how could they do this to a big-timer, as I considered myself?

I sat down and evaluated the situation. Why wasn't I winning, or making a more respectable showing on the tour? I talked it over with my long-time friend Ben Hogan. He listened attentively to my tale of woe, and when I finished, he looked me squarely in the eye and said: "Chi Chi, you're completely out of shape. If I were you, I'd lay off golf for about three months and work myself back into playing condition."

I took Mr. Hogan's advice and went back to Puerto Rico. I laid out a stringent exercising program and vowed I'd stay on it for at least three months. I was up every morning at dawn and running in the sand, at first a mile, then two, and then I stepped it up to three miles. You people who have tried to run in the sand know what I mean when I say this is rough duty.

But just running in the sand wasn't enough. Sure, it strengthened my legs and gave me more wind, but there were other parts of the body that needed tuning, such as the hands. I had read about the great baseball player Ted Williams squeezing rubber balls to build up his hand, wrist, and arm muscles. I bought some rubber balls and carried one with me at all times. When I wasn't doing anything else, I was squeezing the ball. After about a month of this I could feel the power coming back into my swing.

Then there are the shoulder muscles. I got myself a set of bar bells. Man, that first couple of weeks I thought I was going to die, I was so sore and stiff. But, little by little, I got used to lifting the weights, and pretty soon I was able to swing seventy-five pounds around with little exertion. I know, some of you are going to say that lifting weights will make you muscle-bound. This muscle-bound superstition has been disproved by scientific tests which actually show that weight-trained athletes have faster reflexes than the nonweight users.

As you know, golf isn't strenuous enough to keep the body in shape even if it belongs to a pro who hits a thousand balls a day and climbs Pikes Peak on weekends. Swinging a club and walking is kid stuff. It's just not enough to keep fit, much less develop extra strength and endurance. I forget what physical culturist said: "Exercise is of value only if there is enough expenditure of energy to stimulate the heart and lungs. The only exercise of any value must be heavy and sustained long enough to make one winded."

Many of the young players on the tour today spend their off hours doing roadwork and working out in a gym. They have built power into their shoulders and legs, and when they step up on that first tee you know you're going to have your hands full. Of course, Gary Player is the model for this type of golfer. Player was the first golfer to work a full physical education program into his daily routine.

"You've got to hit long all day and every day in tournament play," says Gary. "If your strength fades on the last day, or even in the last hour every day, your accuracy fails, and consequently your confidence and your score." Words of wisdom from this little 160-pounder who has become a giant in the golfing world.

Gary uses a vigorous all-around bar-bell program to keep in shape, with special attention to hands and legs. He'll do eighty floor dips, run a mile, or skip rope for five minutes every day of his life.

Jerry Barber, who came on in the late 1950s, is another small man who followed a physical education program to advantage. Jerry, who weighs about 135 pounds, wasn't doing too well on the tournament tour until he decided to increase his strength. Every morning he would do fifty push-ups, run a mile, and work out with twenty-five-pound dumbbells. For his grip he tied a weight on each end of a broomstick and rolled it up his arms until his forearms screamed for mercy. He was voted Golfer of the Year in 1961, and he attributes it all to his body-building program.

I have always maintained that the grip is the most important part of physical training. But there are also the muscles in the back of your arms and legs, which are involved in pushing off. And then there are the back muscles that need tuning all the time. There's an old saying, "When your legs go, you're finished." It's surprising how strong you do feel when your legs are strong.

As everyone knows, in the golf swing you use your body as a unit. But when such muscles as those in the forearms or the back or the twisting muscles of the sides are weak, you have to strengthen them, as well as the grip and leg muscles.

Another advantage of staying in shape is that when you feel strong your concentration becomes more keen, you feel more aggressive, and become better attuned mentally to face any test.

A good many of the younger players have gone to vitamin pills to supplement their daily diet. I haven't gotten around to that yet, but I may if I feel I'm deficient in any of these vitamin departments. Anyhow, we'll discuss diet and vitamins in the next chapter.

A number of the new teaching professionals emphasize the importance of power. They tell their students, "Slug the ball as far as you can and forget about accuracy." I can understand this, since putting everything into a shot helps stretch out and strengthen those muscles you need in your game. Then, once you've got the power swing down pat, you can work on your accuracy.

I know what a lot of you are saying at this point. You're saying, "I haven't got time to do all this stuff—after all, I'm busy on the job all week." Well, there's another form of exercise called isometrics that can help. And isometrics take only about fifteen minutes a day.

Isometric exercises are those that hold muscles in the state of static position (in a tensed position). They *do not* involve motion of any kind. Physical education experts first became aware of such exercises by watching jungle animals in a zoo. Although these animals don't have the opportunities to exercise that they did in their natural environment, they still manage to stay in shape. They do this by using their own version of isometrics, such as stretching.

Many people who don't understand the basics of isometrics may think that this is some newfangled idea that's both complicated and confusing. On the contrary, a series of simple, nonstrenuous isometric exercises, designed to strengthen the golf muscles, can be performed in a daily program lasting less than fifteen minutes.

As with any other exercise program, your isometrics regime

should start slowly and increase gradually over a period of time. Then, once you get into the swing of things, you can start off with the light exercises and gradually hit the heavier ones.

A few tips before I give you the basic exercises: *Do not* maintain tension for more than fifteen seconds for the lighter exercises and for more than eight seconds for the heavier ones. During the first three or four minutes use about half of what you feel is your full strength. Gradually increase effort until, after three weeks, you can go all-out.

First, the grip: Hold a wedge straight up for five seconds with the arm fully extended. Then, hold the wedge pointed down for five seconds with the arm extended. Keep pressure on the grip. Then do the same with the other arm. Next, hold the wedge straight out with the thumb and forefinger, keeping the elbow against your side. After holding this position for about five seconds, roll the wrist so that the palm faces the floor; then roll the wrist so that the palm faces the ceiling. Hold each position about five seconds. Spread the fingers wide and press down on a table with maximum strength for about fifteen seconds.

Ankles, instep, and calves: Place the instep of one foot on a step with the other foot about 14 inches behind. Press forward with your back foot while pushing down with the heel. Hold for ten seconds and repeat with each foot five times.

Knees, hips, and legs: Do deep knee bends with the back straight and the thighs parallel to the floor. Extend the arms and hold for four seconds. Do this five times.

Back and neck muscles: Turn head and torso to one side as far as possible and take a deep breath. Hold this position for fifteen seconds. Then turn to the other side. Repeat three times.

Extend both arms in a doorway and push with maximum strength for five seconds. Put head against the wall and push with maximum effort for five seconds.

There are many other forms of exercise that are standard in any gym. Hanging from parallel bars will do wonders for the back muscles. There is weight lifting, bike riding, also part of standard gym equipment. You can do push-ups, sit-ups, toe touching, side bends. All of which will help develop those muscles so sorely needed on the golf course.

While I have dwelt on physical attributes in this chapter, I don't mean to exclude the mental side. When you're in top physical shape, you have much greater nerve control, coolness, and all the other psychological advantages needed to give you the edge under fire.

And this is a fact: No golfer, no matter how good, ever reached his potential without fulfilling the all-out capacity his body would be capable of with the adoption of a strength-building exercise program. As we all know, a well-disciplined athlete in good shape will beat the other kind any day. In the meantime, I'll see you on the beach.

24 DIETING YOUR WAY TO BETTER SCORES

Someone once observed, "All the world loves a fat man." Well, I'm sure whoever it was wasn't thinking about the sports world. Oh, sure, you like everyone, including fat people. But if I had to choose a partner in a high-stakes golf game, I certainly wouldn't pick a guy who wears an inner tube around his waist.

Of course, there have been a few heavy fellows on the tour. People like Porky Oliver and the great Englishman Ted Ray. But, on the whole, the average pro golfer is a neat, trim person who knows the value of staying in shape. And you can't stay in shape if you eat too much.

Dieting is one of the most important parts of our everyday life. And it boils down to a simple solution: Overweight is caused simply by overeating. If you take more calories into your body than you dispose of, you're bound to gain weight.

Being a little guy (126 pounds), I have never known the miseries of dieting, as some of my touring pals have. Even so, I never overindulge. Every day of the year, whether I'm in a tournament or relaxing at Dorado Beach, I eat the same breakfast—orange juice, two eggs, prepared in various ways; and toast. I *do* change my beverage. When I'm relaxing at home, I drink coffee, but when I'm playing in a tournament I always have hot chocolate made with milk. The reason for this is that coffee flares up on me at times, makes me jittery. Through the years I have found that I'm much more comfortable over a putt if I stick to hot chocolate.

The only thing that varies drastically between when I'm in tournament play and when I'm just hanging around is my lunch. When I'm competing, I never touch a thing for about two hours before I go on the golf course. If I'm at home, I'll have a light sandwich and a cold drink of some kind. Again, experience has taught me that you can't eat a meal and go out there and compete under pressure. In the first place, being under pressure steps up the adrenalin flow and hampers the digestive system. I never go into tournament play with anything on my stomach.

Dinner is a different matter. Regardless of where I am or what I'm doing, I really eat at dinnertime. But you'd be surprised at what I eat. I like boiled things, such as stews. I like casseroles and roast beef and cottage cheese and custards. I'm partial to light things that give me vitamins but don't drain my strength just in the eating of them. Steaks? Sure, I like steaks, but only once in a while. The cholesterol in steaks, potatoes, gravy, and other heavy foods outweighs the momentary pleasure you get from eating them.

There have been some pretty big stars who found they were eating themselves right off the tournament tour. Billy Casper was one, and Phil Rodgers was another. Both were literally butterballs and weren't doing so well on the tour. Both went on diets, and the recovery was unbelievable. Casper won the U.S. Open and some $120,000 in 1966 after shedding pounds. In that same year Thin Man Rodgers won twice and today is one of the fine exponents of the game of golf.

The golfer who maintains the proper weight for his height and age will not only look and feel better; he'll be able to swing with easy freedom and balance. Excess weight has ruined many a good round, causing players to tire mentally and physically on the finishing holes.

Of course, the person who is too heavy and wants to swing the loose stick *has* to go on a diet. Proper dieting is the best—in fact, the only way—to shed unwanted pounds. The idea of any weight-losing diet is to reduce your calorie intake to the point where it is less than your calorie output. But exercise, such as playing golf, does speed the operation.

The golfer who plays a round of golf (on foot) on a 6500-yard course puts in about five miles. Even with a caddie, he should burn off about 350 calories. If he carries his own clubs, he uses up at least 500 calories. And if he's on the practice tee before a round, he can use up approximately another 150 calories, depending on how long he stays on the tee.

So if you go into a diet program of about 1000 calories a day (this is a seven-day deal), you should be in pretty good shape at the end of a month. That is, of course, if you're overweight by about twenty-five pounds. If you play golf four times a week and restrict yourself to the 1000-calorie diet every day, you should lose two pounds a day. It's safe to lose up to twenty pounds during a ten-week period. I know this seems like a slow way to take it off, but if you can tell me of a better way, I'll be happy to listen, since I've gone over this thing with my family doctor.

So-called crash diets are a no. Hardly anyone who starves himself into shape maintains the lowest poundage he reaches. Hey, man, this is only natural. We people on the golf circuit, whether international or local, live off the fat of the land. It's very easy to succumb to the 19th hole and other enticements along the way. And eating habits just aren't changed that quickly.

Watching calories in your everyday mode of living is good, but it is also possible to lose weight by consuming various diet foods on the market. However, once a person gets down to his proper weight, he should go off the diet bit and merely maintain his weight by eating properly at regular meals. In either case, dieting will help you get into better eating habits and thus maintain your best weight.

Now, to get down to the nitty-gritty of this chapter. I'm going to outline a couple of days on the diet trail, with the calories involved. You can take it from there.

BREAKFAST: One half grapefruit with no sugar. Cereal with three ounces of whole milk and one teaspoon of sugar. Coffee or tea with no cream or sugar. The biggest item of the four is the cereal, which contains 110 calories. The milk goes 60, the grapefruit 25, the sugar 20, and there's no score for the beverage.

LUNCH: A meatless vegetable soup (70 calories), a pineapple salad (40), cottage cheese with lettuce (170), one slice of whole-wheat bread (55), one teaspoon of butter (25), one half honeydew melon or cantaloupe (50), and an eight-ounce glass of skim milk (95).

DINNER: Tomato juice (50 calories), one thick lamb chop with the fat removed (200), string beans (25), spinach (ugh and 15), cucumber and lettuce salad (15), and baked apple with no added sugar (50). And you have nothing to pay for the coffee or tea without milk or cream.

That's a one-day shot (according to my good doctor), and it adds up to about 1000 calories. You must understand that this leaves nothing for the 19th-hole goodies. However, if you want good results, you're just going to have to show a little will power and fend off the good-time Charlie who wants to kill you with kindness, such as Scotch, gin, or mixed drinks.

Here's another day's regimen on the lose-weight circuit:

BREAKFAST: One fresh peach or large pear (60 calories), prepared cereal with three ounces of whole milk (170), one teaspoon of sugar (20). Again, no weight charge for coffee or tea *if* you don't use cream or milk.

LUNCH: A two-egg omelet (or two scrambled eggs) with a half teaspoon of butter contains 172 calories; lettuce and tomato salad (25), one slice of white bread (65) with a half teaspoon of butter (13), and a baked apple with no sugar (50).

DINNER: One glass of grapefruit juice (50), one breast of chicken, roasted or broiled (160), small portion of broccoli (15), summer squash (15), one slice of melba toast (40), a cabbage and carrot salad (40), and one cup of custard (110).

Sure, I could give you many other menus, but you can find them in any diet book and I won't bore you with the details. Just remember—if you want the best of everything on the golf course, you've got to get down to your playing weight. I know it won't be too easy for you heavyweights, but think of the satisfaction when you pull it off!

25 EQUIPMENT

Every year someone comes out with an innovation that is absolutely guaranteed to lower your score, put more boom into your drives, keep you calm, cool, and collected, and, I guess, even put hair on your chest. How many of these "new deals" do you need? In this chapter we won't fool around with the offbeat material. We're going to stick strictly to basics.

I guess the latest controversial item on the market is the "amazing" graphite-shaft club. This is supposed to add some 25 yards to your tee shots. Some pros are using it and swearing by it. Others wouldn't touch it with a ten-foot pole, saying they can't control the club. Let's look into the situation.

Sure, you get more distance. This is achieved simply because the shaft weight is two ounces less than that of the conventional steel shaft, which allows for a heavier head. The result is that the lighter shaft increases the clubhead speed while the heavier head delivers more power.

As with any new gadget on the golfing market, the graphite shaft has brought controversy into the game. The United States Golf Association (USGA) is investigating the shaft with the possibility of establishing controls on it. The USGA announcement in May 1973 stated:

> The USGA fears the recent aerodynamic developments in ball dimpling and the introduction of the graphite shaft may render existing distance controls inadequate. Consequently, the USGA has recently instituted a series of tests, both indoor and outdoor, to determine the extent of the effect, if any, of these developments on distance. Over the next few months, the tests will be conducted mechanically, although there will be some tests by golfers as well.
>
> As the ruling body of golf in the United States, the USGA is prepared to take action if its tests show a distance bonus has been achieved through these new developments. At present, the distance of the golf ball is controlled by size, weight, and initial velocity restrictions. There is no comparable restriction on the clubs.

Some say the USGA will bar the graphite shaft. Others say it won't because of the possibility of law suits. As most of you can remember, when steel shafts replaced the wooden variety, and when fiber glass and aluminum shafts were introduced, there were no controls put on them. But they added nowhere near the distance that graphite has.

Even as the controversy rages over the graphite shaft, still another innovation has been added. It's the carbon-graphite shaft called Carbonite. The Carbonite shaft is claimed to be designed so that you still get the distance bonus but remain in better control of the golf shot.

The Carbonite manufacturers claim their club is closer to the conventional steel model than the graphite. They also say that the new combination of graphite and carbon gives more control because of less whip, yet also gives the greater distance on the tee shot.

The Carbonite shaft retails for about $65 for the shaft alone. If you want your own clubs reshafted, it will cost you about $85 per club. But, remember, you just might be blowing your money out the window in case the USGA turns thumbs down on this new "power play" in golf.

Another angle along the equipment line is "swingweight." This is one of golf's mysterious names, although it need not be. Swingweight merely is a helpful passage toward getting clubs that best fit your physical build. Thus, its importance lies in its role as a standard of club measurement, and a check as to whether or not each individual club in your set swings the same way.

A club's swingweight is computed on a special scale which relates the weight of the clubhead to that of the balance of the club. With the toe of the clubhead pointed down, the club is put on the scale and a reading is taken. This reading is the swingweight of your club.

A professional can tell, through the use of the scale and without even seeing the person swing, whether the clubs are particularly suited to his game. This is because swingweights fall into three distinctive classes—light, medium, and heavy. Naturally, if you're a big person you don't want a light club. Just the opposite is true if you're a little guy like me.

Swingweight scale measurements fall into a letter-number combination. The letters range from A through E. The numbers go from 0 to 9. The A and B weights are much too light and are designed for the junior set. The E weights are much too heavy for general use. Nearly all clubs fall between the C–0 and D–9 figures.

What makes the swingweight most important is the advantage of having all your clubs the same. This gives you a certain "feel" that you wouldn't have if all your clubs were of varying weights.

WHIPPY CLUB

Thus, the golfer can go ahead and use his normal swing with all his clubs without any adjustments in his swing.

The degree of shaft flex is closely associated with swingweight. As everyone knows, a player must be able to swing firmly enough so that the shaft flexes on its way into the shot. This is what happens: As the hands go into the impact area, their forward progress slows to allow the wrists to uncock. During this time, if the golfer is using the proper swingweight and shaft flex, the force of the swing and the slowing of the hands will cause the clubhead to lag behind the shaft just before impact. Then, at the last second, it will lunge into the ball, giving you the most power at point of impact and on through the shot.

As you go through your clubs—two iron to nine iron—the shorter the club the heavier the clubhead. Thus, the two iron, although longer, will have a lighter clubhead than a three iron. To maintain that matched "feel," as the clubheads become heavier the shafts must become stiffer to compensate for this extra weight. This is the only way you can come up with a matched set of clubs.

It is only natural that the bigger, stronger golfer will be able to swing heavier swingweighted clubs with their stiffer shafts and still get the proper shaft flex. On the other side of the coin, the woman, or the senior, or the once-a-week golfer should use clubs with lighter swingweights and more flexible shafts. In both cases every golfer should be able to "feel" the clubhead as he or she swings through each shot.

Most men will find swingweights from D–0 through D–5 suitable, while most women fall into the C–4 through C–9 bracket.

But now you're saying, "How do I know if I've got the feel of the clubhead?" Very simple. If the clubhead feels as though it were on the end of a fishing rod on your backswing, then your swingweight is too light or you're using a shaft that's too flexible.

On the other hand, if your clubhead feels as if it were on the end of an iron pipe, your clubs are too heavy or your shafts are too stiff.

Another way to tell if you're using the proper clubs can be found in the result of most of your shots. For instance: If you slice a lot or top the ball many times, you're using too heavy a swingweight. You're slicing because you're not strong enough to flex the shaft properly at impact. In other words, the clubface will still be open at point of impact. Of course, you still might be getting good distance, but you'll be hitting to the right consistently.

If your clubs are too light, you'll have the tendency to hook. This is because your shaft is too flexible, which causes the clubface to close at point of impact. Of course, swing faults also may be causing these errors, and the only way you're going to get this straightened out is a visit to your local professional.

There are a couple of ways to alter swingweight. One is to add weight to the clubhead, and the other is to take away weight from the clubhead. Then you can always change shafts.

However, before you go about altering your clubs, it's always best to get the advice of an expert. The average golfer can't tell solely by feel. He has to see what's happening to his shots and go from there.

Most clubs are made too flat—in other words you have to bend over too far to hit the ball. This is bad because it throws off your timing and you therefore lose distance and accuracy. Naturally, a big man's clubs should be more upright.

All golf ball manufacturers make the 100- and 90-compression golf balls. And most make a thin-skinned ball and a thick-skinned one. The thin-skinned ball is for the guy who knows he's going to hit the ball on the sweet spot most of the time. The thick-skinned ball is designed for the weekender who has a tendency to cut the cover through misguided swings. Of course, if the high-handicapper could spend more time on the golf course, I'm sure he'd be able to use the same ball as the professional.

The new type of ball dimpling is another factor to be considered. A certain manufacturer came out with a square, shallow dimple. Then another offered the larger round dimples. On the basis of the findings of their testing laboratories, these manufacturers claimed longer shots and more control over the ball.

Some of the pro people are currently trying out these new balls and have come to the conclusion that the deeper dimples have a tendency to "rise" the ball, get it higher into the air. I guess this would be an advantage when going with the wind, but what if you're bucking the wind? However, it all evens out in the end.

The solid ball is another innovation that seems to be catching on across the country. This ball has the tough skin good for week-end play and seems to have the desired carry we're all looking for. And since the compression ratio is about 90, it is proving a boon to the high-handicapper.

The guys get bigger, the equipment get better, and the "new" is keeping the USGA busy, so let's stick to the basics. After all, all the gimmicks in the world won't solve any problems unless you're able to handle all the shots in the bag. Practice, and practice alone, will get you where you want to be in the golf world. See you on the practice tee.

26 MINI-TIPS: A PICTORIAL REVIEW

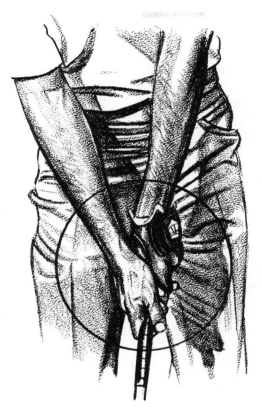

FIRST: THE GRIP

1.   The grip on your club has much to do with your shots. In wet weather the leather grip becomes slick. The rubber-processed grip may be too harsh on your hands in dry weather. Size and thickness are important. So if you're having hand problems because of your grip, check out some new ones in the pro shop. It could make a big difference. . . .

2.   A good grip is essential to a good swing in golf. I use the overlapping grip, better known as the Vardon grip. This grip should be firm but never tight. Try to imagine that you're holding a little bird and you don't want it to get away. The tightness should disappear and the firm hold should take over. . . .

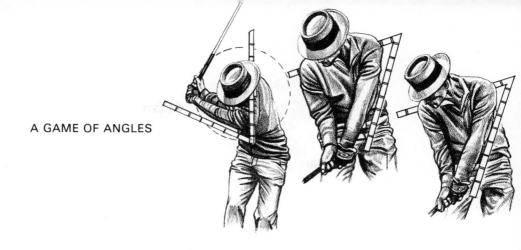

A GAME OF ANGLES

WHERE THE EYES SHOULD BE

3.   Since most of us haven't got the loot to go out and buy a set of clubs every couple of weeks, it's a pretty good idea to keep our own clubs in good shape. Furniture polish will do wonders for the woods, and some lukewarm water will take care of the irons. Also, head covers cost comparatively little and protect big. Make it a part of your game to keep your equipment in good shape. . . .

4.   For you youngsters who have a golf career in mind, don't wait. There are many fine young pros on the tour. In fact, fourteen of the top forty are under thirty years old. So if you're really interested, get going . . . nothing is more rewarding than being a successful pro golfer. . . .

5.   Keeping your eye on the ball is important in any game but never more so than in golf. Where do you look on the ball as you go into your swing? The best rule to remember here is that you imagine you're shooting pool and you want to hit the ball where the cue strikes the spot on the back side of the cue ball. . . .

THE IRONS . . . START . . .

6.   In taking your stance, there are basic maneuvers you must try for each time. You place the clubhead, set your hands properly on the handle, get your feet in the proper position, and set your head and body the way they feel the most comfortable. Your position before swinging is most important since this is where you should be at point of impact. Any slight error at the start of your swing could enlarge into a real bomb. . . .

7.   Trying to concentrate on too many things at one time has ruined many a promising golfer. One of the most important parts of the game is your backswing. I use about a three-quarter backswing, which is the one that allows me the most body turn. I know, this is one of the most difficult parts of the game and requires a lot of practice. However, once you get the proper backswing, forget it. It'll just come naturally from there on in. . . .

. . . AND FINISH

8.   We pros practice constantly. Many amateurs work hard at their game, too. But the high-handicapper usually makes the mistake of practicing the shots that he does best. Of course, this is a bad deal. If you want a well-rounded game, you've got to have all the shots in the bag. And it's the weak points that need to be honed to make you a strong winner. . . .

9.   I use only about 90 per cent of my energy on most of my drives. This, of course, gives me greater accuracy and reserves my strength for the time when I would need a king-size one. However, I would recommend to the tyro that he go all out on his tee shots when he's beginning. It's always better to backtrack than to develop a lazy swing that you can't build up in the future. . . .

THE COMPLETE IRON STORY

10.   When you're undecided about club selection, always use the more lofted, or shorter, club. This way you can use the full swing, and the higher shot will keep you out of a lot of trouble, since usually there are more hazards behind a green than in front. Also, if the lofted shot is long, it won't run as far as when you use the less lofted club. . . .

11.   In this book I have harped on practice, practice, and more practice. As in any form of endeavor, practice makes perfect. However, if you feel that your practicing is doing little good, see your pro. You may be doing something incorrectly, in which case practice will do more harm than good. . . .

WOOD ROUGH PLAY

YOU FACE LEFT OF YOUR TARGET
TO COMPENSATE FOR THE PULL OF THE ROUGH.

12. The touring professional golfer's life is one of constant tension, traveling, and practice. Many tournaments are played in exhausting heat that drains the body reserves. Some players munch candy bars. Others eat pure sugar. And there's Al Geiberger, who takes along a couple of peanut butter sandwiches on every round. Me? I like a sip of honey now and then. However, to the high-handicapper who doesn't have to play, if the conditions aren't favorable, come back another day. . . .

13. When lining up any shot, think about what you'd *like* to do with it and put everything else out of your mind. Mentally, you should always think on the positive side. And, one thing for sure, play your own shot and forget about your partners. Believe it or not, more rounds are won by thinking positively than by worrying about what *not* to do. . . .

14. So you can't get out to the course as much as you'd like. Solution: Grab a rake or a hoe and swing it around the house. Do a few sit-ups and push-ups. Walk a little each day. You can't sit on your pants every day and then hop out to the golf course on weekends and expect to break par. A little exercise will make life more enjoyable and lower that golf score. . . .

OFF THE LEFT HEEL FOR DISTANCE

15. To do any kind of job requires basic tools in any occupation. Golf is no different. Basic requirements include clubs, shoes, and bag. Since all persons are different, we need different basics. Any qualified pro is the key to your selection of golf equipment. See him. He'll be delighted to help you out. . . .

16. Golf is an individualistic undertaking, and no two golfers, pro or otherwise, do the same things the same way. If you study the leading pros in the game today, you'll see various details that just don't mesh. However, if you notice them at point of impact, you'll find they're doing basically the same thing. So don't try to copy anyone. Just do your own thing in your own way, but be sure you're doing it right at point of impact. . . .

AND THE SOLID LEFT WALL FOR POWER

17.　Stance is of the utmost importance in golf. I would recommend that on your longest shot—the drive—you use no stance where your feet are wider apart than your shoulders. But you should use a stance that allows you the biggest body turn. Of course, this will take some experimentation and practice. The main thing is that you use the same stance on the same shot each time. . . .

18.　We all know that the timid soul isn't the good golfer. However, the cocky guy hasn't much more chance. You've seen the one who uses a lesser club on a shot because he wants to show off his strength. Well, this doesn't work most of the time, and he usually winds up short of his target. Play your own game and use whichever club you think is the proper one, regardless of your partners' reactions. Remember, he who laughs last laughs best. . . .

HEAD AND EYES DOWN

THE FINISHED SWING

19.   The strong left side is a must in my game. And the funny thing about this is that you don't have to be on a golf course to perfect it. Just place the left side of your body—shoulder, hip, leg, and foot—against any doorjamb as tightly as possible. Then position your hands as though you had a club in them and start your backswing as you normally would. It's tough at first, but soon you'll get the feel and your worries will be over. . . .

20.   Some golfers talk, others chew gum, others just keep on the move. What I'm getting into is tension and the curing of same. Whatever the cause, tension plays a large part in all our games, and it strikes without notice. The only thing I can tell you is to stay calm and find out what's best for you under these conditions. And remember, we all feel tension at one time or another. . . .

21.   The rules of good housekeeping were never more important than on a golf course. A golf course is an expensive item and you can help keep it that way by practicing a few do's: replacing divots, repairing ball marks on the green, picking up loose bits of paper, and never banging your club down on a green. . . .

OFF THE RIGHT FOOT FROM THE SAND

22. A colorful golfer is a boon to the game; a clown is a disgrace. So learn to control yourself when anyone else is shooting. The colorful guy will always have the right thing to say at the time. The clown is a nuisance and a boor and particularly embarrassing to his playing partners. As in the game of life, control is the word for it. . . .

23. Slipping and sliding when you're getting into your swing may be caused by stubby or clogged spikes on your shoes. This is especially true in wet weather when the grass and mud will build up on your spikes. Keep your spikes long and clean and you'll have that solid feeling that is conducive to hitting the ball on the nose. . . .

24. And, speaking about crowded courses and less time on our hands today, don't let your anxiety build into an uncontrolled thing. Golf is a fun game and should be treated as such. So don't expect to be home for dinner at five o'clock if you're teeing off at two. Play it cool and give yourself plenty of time. . . .

25. Like bowling, golf is often offense. You can't expect any help from teammates, and everything you do is strictly a you-yourself effort. So approach the game with an open mind. The right mental picture will bail you out on many a hole. . . .

26. You don't have to rush out and buy a complete set of expensive clubs as soon as you decide to take up the game. A set of six inexpensive clubs will do the job until you decide to become serious about the game. A good starter set should include a three wood, a three, a five, a seven, and a nine iron, and a putter. . . .

27. "Fore" is the warning word in golf that's becoming almost extinct as the years roll by. More play and less time is the excuse used by the non-yellers. But if you've ever been hit by a flying shot, you'll never forget how to holler, "FORE!". . . .

28. Your putter is your best chipper! Shocked? You wouldn't be if you used it on some of those shots just off the fringe. With a little practice you'll find that you have much more control over your putter on a shot like this than over a nine, eight, or seven iron. . . .

THE PITCH "FLOATER"

AND FINALLY . . .

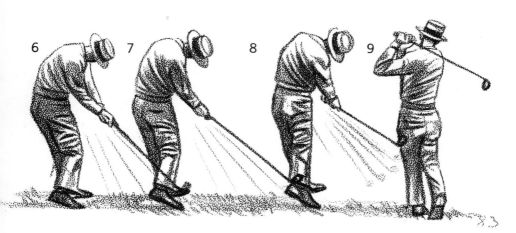

. . . THE COMPLETE SHOT

29. If you're having trouble keeping your balance when you swing the power clubs, try turning your left toe in . . . sort of pigeon-toed. Many golfers turn their left toe toward the target, but if you're slight like me, try turning your left toe in. You'll be surprised at the feeling of solidity it gives you. . . .

30. Tom Weiskopf, among others, has been accused of being too touchy on the golf course. In Tom's defense, I must say that this

is an outgrowth of some happenings over the years that have conclusively affected the outcome of many tournaments. We pro golfers really appreciate the adulation we have received over the years. But all we ask is that we be treated as you would want to be treated if you were hitting those shots. . . .

27 CONCLUSION

Well, that's it! If you've absorbed everything I've been over and have spent some considerable time on the practice tee, you should be showing improvement in your game. When we started, I said I'd knock ten to fifteen strokes off your score—that is, if you're a 90 shooter. So just to make sure you haven't been practicing the wrong way, we'll go into a short review of the basics.

First, the grip. As I said, I use the Vardon, or overlapping, grip. But, as I also said, the baseball grip and the interlocking grip have their points, too, and if you feel more comfortable with them, go ahead. After all, if you're not comfortable in any phase of the game, you might as well forget it. Another important reminder on the grip: Not too tight and not too loose.

Next on the basics is the stance. Remember, there are three types . . . the square, the closed, and the open. I use the open (drawing my left foot back slightly from the line of flight). However, I recommend the square stance for most of you. And your feet should be no farther apart than your shoulders. Of course, as you use the more lofted clubs, you will decrease the width of your stance. As for the head and eyes, I always keep my head about six inches in back of the ball when I'm using my driver. Again, the average player would do all right if his head was directly over the ball. The pocket of the elbows should be pointing skyward, *not at each other!* You should be a little more on your heels than on the balls of your feet. On the long shots your left knee should be pointing in at point of address. The feeling of good balance is important in your stance.

The basic fundamentals of the take-away are smoothness and the complete lack of hurry. This take-away (backswing) is the first movement in a grooved swing. In other words, move the clubhead the same each time and soon it will become automatic. As you progress on the backswing, your weight will swing from 50–50 to about 75 or 80 per cent to your right foot. The left heel may leave the ground as you near the top of the backswing, but not too much. First the waggle, in which you get comfortable over the ball and get good balance. Then the movement goes like this: hands, arms, shoulders, and then the hips. The left arm should remain as firm as possible.

As you go into the downswing, your hips initiate the movement. The shoulders should act as a pendulum and the hands should *not uncock* until point of impact. Both legs should coordinate the action: When the player's hands are approaching the hip level on the downswing, the hips are on their way to facing the target at the completion of the swing. While the right leg is pointed in, the left leg should remain rigid as it takes the full weight of the body at point of impact. I use about 85 per cent of my power on most shots. If you use more than that, you have a tendency to spray your shots.

So, in parting, all I can say to you is stay loose and practice. As you know, there's no substitute in any sport for practice. If you have followed the theme throughout the lessons, you should be surprising a lot of your friends in those two-dollar Nassaus. Good luck!